MW01043392

"WE WILL NEVER BE
STRANGERS"

9-21-2020

Warren

Dedication

For my wife Yolanda…
who is no stranger to me.

1977 - _ _ _ _

Warren Woodberry
St. John's Antigua
West Indies

A personalized copy of this book can be purchased
from the author

Yin

This passive element in dualistic philosophy representing the female qualities of darkness and cold in constant interaction with it's opposing principle (Yang)

The element in dualistic philosophy representing the male qualities of light and heat in constant interaction with it's opposing principle (Yin)

Light gives way to darkness
Reason to feelings
Yang to Yin
The head to the heart.

For We Are Strangers

By: Warren Woodberry

"A word of caution: This is not a book for a person that merely follow a religion and have no spiritual convictions of their own — because the book accuses, tries and passes judgment on most preconceived notions of established religions, both Christian and others.

It is an emergency book for relationships in trouble. However, I am convinced that if this book is read and taken to heart by couples at the *beginning* of their relationship, it becomes a preventative measure."

D. Gisele Isaac
Writer, poet, screenwriter
St. John's Antigua
West Indies

THE NEED TO LOVE

IS GREATER

THAN EVER

Every idea is an indictment. It offers itself for belief and if believed, it is acted upon unless some other belief outweighs it.

Many ideas grow better when transplanted into another mind than in the one where they sprang up.

Oliver Wendell Holmes

In **FOR WE ARE STRANGERS** Warren Woodberry has confronted– and I use that word very deliberately– the oldest problem on earth. The battle between the sexes grows more intense by the minute, leading to the disaster of estrangement between the two essential units of life and humanity.

Woodberry explores, not with a view to reach a truce, as a negotiated settlement. He does so in an ontological sense. That is, to find a way of being, to go beyond "the injustices of the past" "the shams" that substitute themselves, "denying sight in the darkness for generations to come."

It is to uncover our deception of man to woman, and woman to man that Woodberry turns his laser beam with an uncanny persistence. The end result is a roller coaster ride, hurtling through the past, shattering preconceptions along the way. This exciting and sometimes tremulous journey lands the reader on new ground. Ready to begin anew the old relationship of man to woman, without the baggage which centuries of domination of woman by man has left as romanticized carcinogens. It is a must read. A necessity for a new way of being in a new millennium.

TIM HECTOR
Noted Caribbean Literary Critic
Editor of The Outlet Newspaper
St. John's, Antigua, West Indies

It is time for us, male and female, to stop the power struggle. **"We are both guilty"...** therefore a selfless love between us, is truly the only way to restore the disturbed balance in the forces of the universe. Warren Woodberry's book is an exceptional prose written in clear concise, repetitive mantras causing one to reflect, mull over, and savor deeply the truths captured within its pages.

We have heard them before. We have sought to understand them before. We only need to act upon them. It is of great urgency that man and woman come to the forum of discussion with open minds and hearts. Time is running out and we are, unfortunately, still strangers.

A serious read...anyone interested in walking as an equal with their partner should definitely obtain a copy.

Nykia Caffe
Writer and Poet
The Daily Observer Newspaper
St. John's Antigua, West Indies

Copyright © 2002 by Warren Woodberry
Art copyright © 2001 by Warren Woodberry

All rights reserved

*This book printed and bound by **BookMasters, Inc***
Mansfield Ohio. USA

All rights reserved. No part of this publication may be reproduced or transmitted in
any form or by any means, electronic or
mechanical, including photocopy,
recording or any other information storage and retrieval system, without the prior
permission in writing from the author.

ISBN #   0-9720673-0-2

For information on this book
please contact the author.

Warren Woodberry

Email:
forwearestrangers
@yahoo.com

COVER PAINTING BY WARREN WOODBERRY

...For We Are Strangers...

*and I have come to
make love to you...*

CONTENTS

FORWARD 17

FORWARD

FOR WE ARE STRANGERS

A BLUEPRINT FOR THE RECONCILIATION OF THE SEXES

If God found fault with man and woman for having the knowledge of life...then the punishment did not equally fit the crime...as man continues to punish women for his imagined fall from grace.

Are the problems of today created by man as he violently retaliates against woman for being chosen as the vessel of birth?

Is it that some men wish that they had never been born of woman and so vent their anger at her body, soul and mind? How else can one explain the anger that man expresses against women? Man has chosen a religion, but has not chosen to love the reason for his very existence.

PART I

THE FIRST STEP

This journey and book was begun in 1977
in New Orleans, Louisiana

Man and woman have been duped
into living in disharmony...

man and woman have accepted a
religion…

but man and woman have not
chosen to live their life with each
other and God…

FOR WE ARE STRANGERS

We have got to believe that there is a future for man and woman.
Together as lovers…or at least as friends.

With this book an attempt is made to hold out for our future...that the relationship between man and woman will be less strained…less stressful…and less self-destructive…and will follow the path set down by my God…your God...our God.

Every chapter begins and ends with a small but definite step forward. No morbid beginnings showing the futility of human contact…no anger overshadowing and commercializing our differences…no pimping of a gap that seems to be widening between us. Just a frank and open expression and admission of the interaction that we must continue to explore.

More crucial and important than the findings of ancient life...for what effect can their life have on us… if we can ignore each other as we today lay side by side?

More important than the exploration of the sea bottoms…for how can I be moved by the sight of watery life, covered with grains of sand, while you stand naked before me? And more important than the conquest of outer space…for if I cannot love you and you cannot love me_ who share the same image _ what emotion can a creature from another planet invoke in me?

For I would implore *you*...woman...to search the concept of your past or forever burden your daughters, sons and all future generations with your accepted constitution of slavery.

For I will not...cannot...should not...map your escape from the history of your past, as some of you will be content with its interpretation...content with your second class stature...content to play the role of slave and lover...mother and victim.

1
BUILDING BRIDGES

he search for a compatible level of respect, understanding, and love must be rekindled and nourished, and the desire for this state must be given top priority.

For your eyes only.

Man learned his loving of woman while not really learning…and woman returned his love while knowing that he did not really know how to love.

Who is to blame…the one that gave, but did not receive or the one that received, but did not give? Alternatively...do we blame God who had to know that we knew not?

The time and the reason for this time…has at long last arrived. The time for man and woman to stop this gaudy circus of differences where we both sit in the dressing room of the clowns and make up our faces…painting smiles over frowns…and laughter over tears. Painting aggression over fear…and deceit over shame. Hiding our true feeling behind a mask of fear as we paint confusion and distance with a broad-brush.

We paint our faces of pain and then fail to realize that we have created what the other sees...we then fail to take a look in the mirror.

We paint our faces and create images untrue. Between us we build bridges of no return...and we mine these bridges with fuses of self-destruction. We paint what we want the world to see...and then deny it...because it is not what we wanted to portray.

It is time to stop attempting to change God's purpose in uniting us here on this earth. Man and woman...woman and man were meant to complement God's work...not to act as separate entities.

God...my God...your God...our God, did not intend for us to seek audience singularly and turn from one another. It is an affront to God that we seek sexual gratification from experiencing the ecstasy of God while professing no need for this relationship with the very creature that God put on this earth for that purpose...you and I...man and woman...woman and man.

In addition, it is an affront to God that the mating of man and woman would result in such disrespect, anger, violence, rape and murder...for the gift of man and woman was made to the world by God.

We all are guilty of denying God's will...your God...my God...our God.

I have been chosen among men to come forward to take another step __or two or three__ to resolve this dilemma. To remove our self-made differences and to love the physical ones made by this God that we wish to acknowledge.

We must fuse woman's touch with that of man's and attempt to stop this war and rumors of war that has raged between us from the dawn of time. We must remove the borders…tear down the towers of defense…and build bridges to access the connection between you and I…man and woman...woman and man. We must allow tunnels to be dug into our defenses and we must diffuse all land mines that form a protective barrier around us.

We have for too long now pried an ever widening gap between us...

and it must stop!

I am taking the first steps toward this end. I am the first set of human brakes applied to this downhill runaway vehicle. For this vehicle is unloving and uncaring...and will transport us and future generations to our deaths.

Enter not into this world arena as an additional opponent…for we have other things to overcome: disease, sickness, poverty, cruelty, hunger, ethnic cleansing, war and religious persecution.

Enter not this arena with the intention to confuse and belittle man for we need no assistance in this field. Come let us start this journey again...from the beginning…side by side, both sharing the blame for this love-hate relationship.

And while sharing the blame for this confusion...we both must look again.

I will tell you what I saw and you will tell me what you thought that I should have seen. Tell me what you need for me to see…and I will tell you if I see it. We will then replay our lives…and view them through each other's eyes…at last hoping to understand the importance of the task at hand.

Come…let us look deeply into each other's eyes as we attempt to resolve this alienation that we have suffered since the beginning of time. Let us search each other as we seek to find and rekindle the missing and original need that we have let lie dormant for so many years. This need which was instilled in us by the Creator.

In this congested world we attempt to continue to understand things, but not each other. We attempt to acquire, but not inquire...we continue to aspire, but not inspire...and we all pay the price.

It is long past time for me...man...any man...all men...to begin to hear you before we see you, so that we might digest what you say and what you do...before we are swayed and enticed by how you look or feel.

Man did not decide that he needed woman and woman did not decide that she needed man, for if you believe in God...it was the creator who acknowledged that need...and who are we to alter that destiny by hate... violence and division? For I would implore *you*...woman...to search the concept of your past or forever burden your daughters, sons and all future generations with your constitution of slavery.

For I will not...cannot...should not...map your escape from the history of your past as some of you will be content with its interpretation...content with your second class stature...content to play the role of slave and lover...mother and victim.

Some of you have self-chained your mind and body to the concepts of ancient men with ancient minds...and will never be free nor understand your past which binds you here today...rooted to ancient concepts long past their burial day.

But today, among the thinkers in your gender, will be those who will want to know...who will demand to know...who will be burning to know...who will seek to find where man went wrong and where man heard more of the song of the Pagans than he experienced the wisdom of God...your God...my God...our God.

And since the wisdom of God cannot be questioned, it is man and man alone that must now stand trial.

Man must not stand trial as woman once did, with no representation of fairness...with no consideration for love and forgiveness...with no judgement by her peers and by striking the will of God from the witness list by allowing man and man alone to act as judge, jury and executioner.

You and I...man and woman...woman and man...will temper man's verdict with a new love that will sentence man...any man...all men...to help build a better world of compassion and concern...of respect and consideration and of love and understanding between you and I...man and woman...woman and man.

For man can no longer exist as a stranger to woman...any woman...all women...and I will offer these passages as an apology in hopes that you, who are seeking to understand the reason for your burden, will begin this journey back into the teachings of ancient man...hoping to find where God's plan was changed to that of man's.

Hoping that upon your return we will together begin our original journey, side by side according to the will of our creator.

For in your journey to the past you will see, as I have seen that man...any man...all men...has attempted to limit God's hand for the interpretation of selected nations and cultures, and have passed a baton of enforcement to those with power and force. The word of God traveling on chariots of fire and brimstone, deciphered now as history, deciphered now as the hand of God.

Brewed in lands constantly at war...lands constantly at conflict...lands constantly shedding the blood of God's creation...you and I...man and woman...woman and man.

Upon your return from your journey you will decide the deception of ancient men with ancient minds and you will decide if holy land is where man says it is while he desecrates that very same land. You will decide whether mankind has been duped by ancient men with ancient minds as they have placed in the hands of the world, *theirstory of history.*

Their stories...passed from generation to generation...and culture to culture claiming the blessing of God...your God...my God...our God...have attempted to excluded the rest of the world. For in their interpretation, God only blessed one region, one culture and one people...and they would have you believe that, although they existed, no other region was worthy of this blessing. That God...your God...my God...our God, who created the world and the universe, was limited in blessing only one race...one people or one true believer. They would have us believe that God would create a world of non-believers...incapable of knowing their creator.

They would have you believe that the ancestors of Africans were not touched by the hand of God and that they were not the chosen people of God's design.

They would have one believe that the people of Europe were not touched by the hand of God and that they were not the chosen people of God.

They would have one believe that the people of Asia were not touched by the hand of God and that they were not the chosen people of God.

They would teach that they were chosen to bring the word of God to you...the lost...the wicked... the misinformed...the forgotten...and that this word would tie you to *their* history...while demanding that you deny the value of your own.

They would demand that people abandon their pagan beliefs in favor of *their* pagan beliefs. They would demand that everyone abandon a belief in the God of Fire...for belief in *their* God of Fire. That everyone deny that they heard the voice of God in favor of the belief that God only spoke to them.

That everyone abandon their belief in the hereafter, for *their* belief in the hereafter. That the world abandon a belief in the power of their ancestors...for a belief in the powers of *their* ancestors. That *their*story is the only true history of the world, and that since they have condemned woman...the world must condemn woman...any woman...and all women.

They will accept the paganism of the Greeks and mix and match it with *theirhistory* and force feed it to the world through the power of persecution, guilt and military might...but they will not alter the suppression of you...woman...any woman...all women.

And even though today's challenges have changed for us both...as you are no longer measured by your ability to bear man many sons or crush man's grapes or make his wine or make his bread or suffer in silence...change will not come willingly for you.

You will share the confusion as all other unfortunate and unchosen people throughout the rest of the world attempted to abandon their ancient ways to conform to power...as legions of military struck down those who dared believe that God dwelt within us all, and that there were no solitary chosen people of God...your God...my God...our God.

And in your enlightened awareness you will return from this journey and you will direct your mind and your spirit to reject ancient rulings by ancient men and you will finally acknowledge that the world has been deceived.

The will of God lies within us all and ancient men with ancient minds must now take their place on the dust heaps of the obsolete. Their teachings no longer qualify them to rule...allowing them to control our minds and our oneness with God...your God...my God...our God, for we are no longer pawns in their fight to interpret *theirstory* as the history of the world.

God is not limited to *their* interpretation of history, for God is in the history of all men and all women...and it is time to make our individual presence the temple of God, allowing us to communicate with our God wherever we are...not needing far away holy land*s* where they daily bury the bodies of those that come to pray.

Home lands...holy lands...war lands...can you tell the difference?

No longer will rulings be made in your absence by angry men that profess to hear the word of God but yet, attempt to exclude you from the world of love, respect...and equality.

As ancient men with ancient minds emerged from their dreams and hallucinations they said that the world was flat...and that woman was wicked. They said that the world stood still...and that women were unclean. Ancient man said that the sun revolved around the earth...and that women were possessions as were cattle.

Would there not be a reason to question the wisdom of ancient men with ancient minds?

Would you not hear the voices of the church leaders in 1st century CE. ringing in your ears as they declared that "Rather should the words of the Torah be burned than entrusted to woman...whoever teaches his daughter the Torah is like one who teaches her obscenity."

Would not the words of St.Tertullian 155 to 225 CE not painfully remind you of ancient man's view of you when he begged the question "Do you know that you are Eve? The sentence of God on this sex of yours lives in this age: the guilt of necessity lives too."

"You are the Devil's gateway: You are the unsealer of the forbidden tree: You are the first deserter of the divine law: You are she who persuaded him whom the devil was not valiant enough to attack. You destroyed so easily God's image, man. On account of your desserts even the Son of God had to die."

Would you not be shocked that you were to carry the blame for the death of Jesus of Nazareth because of your desserts?

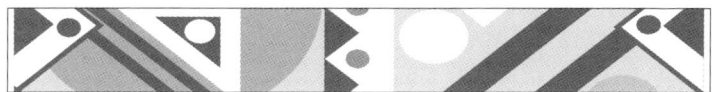

2
TIME TO LEARN

e must look deeply into each other's eyes and not regard contact as an invasion of privacy, but as an attempt to know one another.

We must stop feeling threatened when one attempts to look deeply into our eyes and feel more threatened when one does not. For if we fail to use our eyes to see...what is the point of looking, for are not the eyes the mirror of the Soul?

For love changes as we do…and now we must now learn to love anew…you and I…man and woman…woman and man. For it is impossible to love as our parents loved…for as children some of us were cloaked under their love…and it was not for us to interpret its meaning. For their love was our shield...It was mental and protective...it was not a love for them and them alone...but a love for us.

That love was about healing a wound…leaving on the lights at night and helping with our homework. It was expressed by working a job…providing a home... decorating a tree…giving without receiving… and helping with our prayers at night. There was no passion to their love…as far as we were concerned… for we were but children and were not allowed to witness the method or emotions of our being conceived.

We could witness the new born...the dead and the dying...but not our being conceived. We could watch war...suffering and violence...but not our being conceived. We could watch torture...rape and murder...but not our being conceived. We could watch the mating of the animals...the birds and the bees...but not our being conceived. We could join groups of hate...churches of racism...but could not allow a woman to breastfeed on a train or run naked on a beach. We could watch our ending, but not our beginning.

Something is wrong.

As children we knew not of the stirrings of passion and ecstasy in our parents...for it was not the form of love that we knew...and passion, which at times can drive us all, could not be defined.

And we know that we must never love children with this love. For our love is not for children, and our love is not the image of our parents love. But mature love is a new chemistry...our love is about needs and wants...about longing and desire...about man and woman...woman and man. Our love knows abandonment and lust. Our love is controlled and uncontrollable...it is submission and remission... emotion and unemotion...fantasy and reality...release and suppression...satisfaction and disappointment.

The chemistry of love has baffled the worlds greatest minds.For each mature new love springs from a new a source...one that our parents never knew...or that we never imagined they knew. We must now be allowed to love, free from the restrictions of others interpretations of love.

Man must set the table to allow love to grace its center and that new centerpiece will be freedom for woman to at last love and be loved...both truly and freely.

There are those that question the notion of allowing a woman to be free, just as they question the notion of freedom for others. But why would one desire any other than one that is free? Free to stay...free to go...free to love...free to give.

What man would not benefit from an informed intelligent mate...a mate that would stand side by side to challenge the rest of the world in defending the home, our children and our life?

Is not the home the cave of man and woman.... where we both come to rest and to regain strength for the battle outside? Should not this cave, shared by man and woman...woman and man...be the source of revitalization...peace, harmony and love?

Can one recharge one's soul and body in an atmosphere where the home is perceived as an additional battlefield...where anger, distrust,and hatred dominate and share our bed?

Would a lion retire to his cave after a battle to fight with his mate and cubs?

Would a lion de-fang his mate, making her incapable of assisting in the quality of life for the lair?

Do we have less wisdom than the animals?

Step by step we will try to retrace our steps through our short history knowing that our future can be longer than our past…and that if we get it right, God will allow this to happen...for we have time to learn. And if we cannot immediately find this path...back into the past...lost and buried by man's inhumanity to man and woman...we will begin the steps where we stand today...here and now...together side by side.

For I have traveled your past...back into history, unimpeded by my appearance, and I have traced the confusion of ancient men with ancient minds and have traced the arrogance of those who would deny you your worth in the world today. I have traveled to the first cave of man...and saw his confusion with you... woman...and as I sat there blinded by the fire that you invoke in man...I saw this same blind vision passed to ancient men with ancient minds.

And I traced the beginning of your servitude as it was passed from generation to generation, eventually arriving today at the footsteps of our modern world.... still blinded by the fire of ancient men with ancient minds. And I was ashamed and sped forward...not believing that the myth of woman was to become the law of the land in many countries and among many faiths.Ashamed that the mystery of you...woman... any woman...all women...was allowed to descend below the value of cattle and allowed to descend in value below that of which God had decreed as a gift to the world. For you have sacrificed your life for faith...and for a reward that will never came...for you were the fodder for ancient men with ancient minds. I was ashamed that ancient man with ancient minds would be allowed to write such words and attribute them to God.

Ashamed that man's self manufactured words of God would deny you an audience with your God and declare that man...any man...all men were closer to God and God's image. An image that was created by ancient men with ancient minds...images that were not ever intended to mirror the image of God but was an attempt by ancient men with ancient minds to make God in *their* own image and to reverse the process as the will of God.

Ashamed that ancient men with ancient minds would then declare that you woman were merely an after thought for God...and that originally God had only planned for man and the animals. Ashamed that the world would buy this ridiculous assumption that there was no room at the inn for you woman...any woman... all women.

For I would implore *you*...woman...to search the concept of your past or forever burden your daughters and sons with your constitution of slavery. For I will not...cannot...should not...map your escape from the history of your past...as some of you will be content with its interpretation...content with your second class stature...content to play the role of slave and lover... mother and victim.

I was ashamed that your value plummeted in respect to love...understanding...compassion...or even common decency.

Ashamed of the hoax perpetrated on you... woman...any woman...all women...and of the hoax perpetrated on the world.

And I could travel no further...as I had seen enough. Enough to know that this was a journey, back into your past...that you and you alone must take. A journey to better understand the unsteady platform that lies beneath your feet today.

A platform built on unsound principles in pagan minds that defy the will of God. For when you return from this journey only then will we be able to walk our path together, unfettered by the history of ancient men with ancient minds. For you would have witnessed ancient man's confusion and you would have witnessed the manipulations of the Gnostic as they preached that the body was evil, causing some sects to renounce even marriage and procreation. These men, all void of the knowledge of man...woman...love and God.

Ancient men that set themselves up as the interpreters of God's design. Ancient men so confused by the magic and allure of woman that they would declare that the highest calling of man is to avoid the sight...touch...or carnal of God's creation. Ancient men so confused that they would rather condone and allow man's knowledge of man or innocent children to be more permissible than that of man and woman.

Ancient men so confused by God's creation that many religions will even shun the baring of a woman's hair or her ankle. Ancient men with ancient minds that will declare that the word of God and the blessings thereof should not be read in the presence of a woman with uncovered hair.

God...the God that created this flowing mane to cover the heads of our mothers and sisters would now find that this covering was designated by ancient men with ancient minds as a source of shame. These men, who would be God, attempt to pass judgment on the body parts of woman.

These men, with no authority other than that given by other men, would attempt to deny the blessings of God for women. These ancient men that have blessed murderous rulers...politicians...dictators and members of the underworld, would deny God's blessing to woman with uncovered hair.

Ancient men so afraid of their nature that they would liken the exposure of woman's hair to the exposure of her pubic hair. And these are the men to designate the role of man and woman...woman and man.

46

Ancient men that today scurry from hole to hole...from pew to pew...from church to church...from cathedral to cathedral...from throne to throne...all seeking to cover the uncoverable...all seeking to control the uncontrollable...all seeking to put the genie of power and autonomy back in the bottle as the opening strangles the faithful followers of these ancient men with ancient minds.

Power built on the backs of woman...any woman...all women, as they secured your compliance with manmade laws. Ancient men that ran women into the arms of men that had complied with their ancient teachings and furthered the misunderstanding of the role of man and woman...woman and man.

Men that realized that you...woman...any woman...all women, were confused and believed as taught that women were the cause of the sins of the world. All believing that in some way women were indeed the cause of man being conceived in sin as ancient men with ancient minds would indict your life giving chambers of birth as evil and the source of the separation from God.

Ancient men with ancient minds would then have you bow to the edicts of these ancient men and accept your guilt...your blame...your shame and the fear that God was displeased with your life. And so you would cover your mane of glorious hair that was created by your maker. You would succumb to pagan practices and rulings that would fly in the face of a loving God...and you would follow these ancient rulings by ancient men with ancient minds.

You will have witnessed the myth believers of ancient Greece as they defined the meaningless role of women according to the dictates of their mythical Gods that traveled back and forth from the heavens in flaming chariots, and you will watch these myths about the nature of woman...any woman...all women, persist across time, space, genre and religions.

You will hear myths that Zeus swallowed his wife Metis and gave birth to Athena from his head... thus establishing the principle of the male over the female. You will hear the belief in myths, fables and legends that man desired to reproduce without women and they will surface in some form or another as religious inspiration, ordered by God.

You will see blame laid at the feet of Pandora for bringing the curse to earth BCE...and that "before woman, man had lived apart from evils." You will watch mothers revered for providing great warriors... and if they died in battle, the mothers were honored even more.

In reading the Politics and Ethics you will hear Aristotle defend the subordination of wife to husband with male superior and female inferior.

These myths are then brought forth as the will and directions of God in most religions. Were any of these the real will of God or were they the desires of ancient men with ancient minds?

But these stories will be re-dressed for your wedding hundreds and thousands of years later...and will be found in many religious scriptures today... dictating that these ancient myths from ancient men were to become the *word* of God.

But as you reel in shock you will be fortified to continue your journey as you hear Odysseus praise the act of marriage in poem as he says, " For nothing is finer than this...when husband and wife live together in their home...alike in mind and thought...a great distress to their enemies...but a joy to their friends, as they themselves know best."

I will await your return from this journey for only then can we begin to love anew…you and I…man and woman…child and parent…sister and brother... lover and friend…neighbor and stranger. For only then will you understand.

For each love must spring forth from a new source…burdened by no past…ruled by no ancient rules or myths...not limited by the boundaries of ancient man's attempt to control our minds and our bodies.

Love free from interpretation by others...and by those that seek to suppress love for the sake of control.

We may be told what others think of love…but when we find this love...it will be unique…for it will burn *our* hearts and ours alone. And each fire will be new...never before scorching our lives…and never allowing us to deny its heat.

No distance will dim its memory and no misunderstanding will misdirect its force. This new love between man and woman, will defy all extinguishing factors.

Trial and error cannot be the formula, for loving must be as sure and as inevitable as death and it must be as unavoidable. As we are born to die...we are born to love first, or else, "what is the point?"

For in my journey back into our past I have passed others on the same quest as mine, and we have silently passed each other without speaking...ashamed of what we had seen...and ashamed of the trials and tribulations that man had burdened you and the world with.

Ashamed that some of us had heeded the cry to forsake our wives and children and follow...ashamed that the very essence of our lives with you woman, were to be abandoned while we wandered with the wanderers, marching only to war and to the destruction of man... seeking answers from those who knew not even the questions.

Forgive them for they know not what they do.

Ashamed that some of us abandoned our mothers and fathers...our sisters and brothers...our friends and our neighbors...while we followed. But we now beg the question...follow who...follow where... follow why? For did not God...your God...my God... our God put us where we should be?

For the wanderers still wanders today, seeking God...seeking a home land...seeking a nation...seeking an identity...seeking forgiveness...seeking to be forgiven for wandering and for leading the world astray to wander...and seeking to cause more to wander.

But you woman are not spared this perilous journey as they now bring you into their wars and religious conflicts.

They bring you as a soldier brings extra rations... they bring you for your comforts and not your companionship...they bring you for your labor and not for your wisdom..they bring you for your body...and not for your mind...they bring you for your compliance and not for your strength.

They bring you as prize...as a servant...as a slave...as a whore...as a victim.

These ancient men with ancient minds continuously led us and still lead us astray as they led us into religious wars after religious wars, and only now have some men seen the folly of continuing to follow.

But not following will not spare the women and the children...as they are still the first to suffer as world religions, governments and military leaders bring the wars home and enter each home without a knock.

But those who will not blindly follow these wanderers will build a home with you where you are... and will prize you for the power of your mind...the mystery of your body...the power of your strengths... your words of counsel and the comfort of your arms...as you and man fulfill the journey as directed by your God...my God...our God...leaving others to follow wanderers into the wilderness where the journey has always led. All on a journey to find God who is everywhere. On a journey to a special wall...a special place...a special man made temple...a special mountain or a special statue. All places where wealth is accumulated by the keepers of these "holy places." Places where payment is exchanged for the benefit of the few...where you are told that God will hear you louder and clearer...for a few dollars more.

Imagine that your God my God...our God cannot hear us where we are. Are the acoustics so bad in the world that even God cannot communicate with us where we stand...would one believe the limitations placed on God by ancient men with ancient minds?

And they will continue to declare that God can only be found in the stone and steel buildings that they have built...and that God_who could never be lost_ could only be found through the rituals of their religion.

Your belief in God will be judged by those that insist that you prostate yourself before them and take part in their ceremony of the replacement of God as they combine the power of the church with that of the state to give value to their chosen role. They isolate themselves from woman in rejection of God's gift to the world.

And these political missionaries will then combined the power of church and state to fulfill their attempts to play God. Angry men grit their teeth and pray that the control of you...woman...will return to the bygone days of ancient men as they reluctantly accept the strides made by you...the woman of today...while still plotting your control and return to your dark cave and full length body covering of the past...while visions of 72 virgins dance in their heads.

Be not deceived as they allow you one step forward as they plot your return by steps of two or more. But this time you will not struggle alone...for some men have seen the errors of their past.

Some men will not allow you further deception... for some of us now know that God has not been pleased with this deception of man and woman...woman and man.

And if we are to truly fulfill the wishes of God... my God...your God...our God...then we will finally chart a truer path, void of the conflicts of man against man... religion against religion...scripture against scripture...God against God and man against woman. Once on this new path, will you learn of a division between the teachings of Jesus of Nazareth and the strict Orthodox Jewish laws and customs concerning your rights as a woman and a child of God?

Will you hear that a division was caused because in an effort to acknowledge your rights...even Jesus of Nazareth ran afoul of the teachings of the church and its discrimination of you...woman...any woman...all women?

Will you hear of revelations that Jesus of Nazareth violated the rules of the Essenes, Pharisees and the Sadducees against the equality of women in the church?

Will you hear of the anger by the religious leaders of that time...who were void of the love of women and sought to devalue this need...this acknowledgement of you woman...any woman...all women...and man...any man...all men?

Would you not hear the voices of the church leaders in 1st century CE ring in your ears as they declared that "Rather should the words of the Torah be burned than entrusted to woman...whoever teaches his daughter the Torah is like one who teaches her obscenity."

Would not the words of St.Tertullian 155 to 225 CE not painfully remind you of ancient man's view of you when he begged the question, "Do you know that you are Eve? The sentence of God on this sex of yours lives in this age: the guilt of necessity lives too."

"You are the Devil's gateway: You are the unsealer of the forbidden tree: You are the first deserter of the divine law: You are she who persuaded him whom the devil was not valiant enough to attack. You destroyed so easily God's image, man. On account of your deserts even the Son of God had to die."

Would you not be shocked that you were to carry the blame for the death of Jesus of Nazareth because of your dessert?

And whether you kept your place or not, St. Augustine in 354 to 430 would further ask, "What is the difference whether it is in any woman or a mother, it is still Eve the temptress that we must be aware of in any woman. I fail to see what use woman can be to man, if one excludes the function of bearing children."

Would you not realize that your indictment was written long before the Christian era? Would you not be curious to trace the marriage of paganism with religions of today and their failure to separate fable from myth...legend from reality...mysticism from truth...fact from fiction while adopting wholesale the myth of woman's blame for all the evils of the world.

Would you not pause and count the hands of man as he edited..authorized...altered...abandoned... added...disallowed...included...interpreted... reinterpreted...denied and admitted...and otherwise tampered with the ancient scriptures but would not allow the condemnation of woman to change in content or intent.

Did you not wonder why?

But the treatment of you...woman...any woman...all women...will not find a place or an importance on these agendas or at the center of these meetings.

For your role had been decided centuries before...by ancient men with ancient minds...as they stirred and blended the pot of paganism and the new religions.

And although the hand of man will many times dip his pen into sacred scriptures to reflect the wishes of powerful men...powerful countries...and powerful churches, the pen will not be allowed to dip into the inkwell to alter the indictment of ancient men with ancient minds...against you...woman...any woman...all women.

And you... woman...any woman...all women... must remain as the source of the problems of the world.

How insensitive...how ridiculous...how unGodly.

I would ask that your search halt tomorrow if man found peace in his study of history and religion. But man will not find peace...nor will he find the path to God, for each religious document or artifact found is a new call to war, or of Gods intention to protect one tribe over the other...or one race over the other...or one religion over another...whether it is in the form of a parchment...a scroll...a book...or a letter, and each new discovery is a call to war by some faction, infinitum.

And so your journey must continue.

3
CONFUSION

hen ancient minds scan ancient books that they, and they alone define, how can they show that God's will was to give life to hate…to kill…to scorn…to deny….to not love?

At the time of creation did God, who knows the meaning of all things, plan for misanthropist... misogynist...bigamist and polygamist? Did God not know that man would pretend to seek peace by destroying the peace of others?

In man's ignorance and confusion…his enemy became the enemy of all men...his enemy's God... became his God's enemy…and any man or God could become his enemy. And if man could not select your God…then you were the enemy and death would become you.

Man, in his ignorance and confusion after claiming rejection by God, sought to offer what he thought would appease the creator. He offered virgins…children…the first born and last born. He offered cattle...chickens...crops...slaves...blood... incense…servants and other gifts. Living things...that God had created...were offered dead to the God that created them.

How absurd!

Man prays to...or bows down to walls... crosses...candles...mountains...chalices...animals... stars...moons...planets snakes...child Gods...woman gods...birds...books...temples...ancient documents... the living...the dead and to more Gods, in more different forms, than one can imagine. And not just yesterday but today...and will continue to do so tomorrow. But yet man would still declare himself qualified to be the individual interpreter of God's will, while he continues his hit and miss theory of religion.

Man then declared the church as the temple of God. Gaudy heavy stoned structures...mausoleum in structure...cold, damp and eerie...with artist concepts of heaven hovering above one's head. Muscular men in robes and women nude and overweight...all lounging and floating in the imagined Heavens of man..

Today the church is of glass and chrome...a new tower of Babel, closed to the eyes of God by the security system that now watches our every move. With charlatans in double breasted suits...who arrive from beauty shops in chauffeur driven limousines and wearing Rolex watches.

At what point has man gotten it right?

Man once believed in the Spirit Gods, Goddesses of Earth, Gods of Nature, Gods of Fire, Gods of Water, Gods of the Dead, Sons of God...living Gods that came in chariots from the heavens...Gods of Ancestors and Animal Gods.

Man runs from religion to religion as water runs between the furrows of a newly raked ground, not knowing what furrow to follow. He takes religious views from Buddhism, Hinduism, Greek mythology, Judaism, Christianity, Zoroasterism, Islam, and hundreds of other beliefs. He has mixed them with ancient prophecies and has created a family tree of religions...all related...all connected...all professing one God...and all at war with their neighbor.

Man has left a Christian home and joined Reverend Moon. He has left a Baptist church and joined Jim Jones. Man has written scriptures, and declared that they were the words of God and then modified them to met his financial needs or his desire to be God like. Man will fall on his knees to worship power...money... women...alcohol...and some will sell their God given soul for a vial of drugs.

Some have been raised in a Muslim home, but converted to Christianity while others have abandoned Christian upbringing and converted to Islam. Man has abandoned Christianity and combined it with Voodooism and has no idea which came first, the chicken or the egg. From conversion to confusion as men today wonder what dress to wear...Christian today or Muslim...Hindu tomorrow or Jewish. Conversions from unfounded beliefs to unfounded beliefs. What to follow...who to follow. Maybe one day they will try God.

Mix and match...match and mix...beg and borrow...borrow and beg. An inexact science is this subject called religion.

Neither a beggar or a borrower be...but yet man borrows from all religions...and insist that he knows the way and that his way is pure and free from that of the Pagans.

Is it true that the rosary and the monk came from Buddhism...that the word of Buddha was taught by oral tradition like Christianity until a council of monks collected his teachings two and a half centuries later to put into written form like the apostles did to the teachings of Jesus of Nazareth, forty to 80 years after his death? That nun is from Egyptian nunna...a maiden of the temple of Isis...and that the halo was used by Babylonians artist to deify the heads of mortals?

Is it true that the 25th of December on the Julian calendar is a pagan holiday in honor of the Aryan Sun God Mithera in Sanskrit and Persia, and that in circa 1400 BCE Mithera was born of a virgin in a stable and was worshipped on Sunday and is said to have had a supper in his honor on his last days on earth, and that his followers believe that Mithera ascended to heaven to be with his father.

Did Mithera's followers celebrate with a sacrament of bread and wine, and were bells, candles, incense and holy water used in their celebrations?

That the eating of bread as the symbol of life was a pagan ceremony and that Aristotle taught that bread harbored life many years BC.

Is it a coincidence that believers in Buddha celebrate that he was born of a virgin and had disciples that spread his word...that he preached that freedom from desire and passion were the road to Nirvana and that we should not be prisoners to material things? It is also clear that the status of females is shared among the "ism" religions of Brahmanism, Hinduism, Zoroastrianism, Judaism, Platoism and among Christianity and Islam. And ridicule was also shared as the Brahmins ridiculed the Buddhist while the Orthodox Jews ridiculed the Christians.

Mix and match...match and mix...take your pick.

Religions have mutated to such a degree that they pass themselves on the road and the head does not recognize the tail. Religions have become twisted around in tumblers...mixing early paganism with ignorance and superstitions...able to travel throughout the world with one universal message...that woman is the cause of all sin.

Man has taken fear and brewed it with the ignorance of natural phenomena and announced the birth of religion. Ancient man, whom you would not allow to council you today with the past exposure of their lack of knowledge on most subjects are granted audience to decipher your connection with God. Ancient men with ancient minds declaring their right to interpret our human destiny and to chart our salvation...and to declare that you...woman...any woman...all women, are the cause of the downfall of all humanity.

God has given animals the ability to fear, but not to worship beings or things, but God has given man fears and abilities to choose to worship or not and he has given man the ability to dream and interpret that dream as reality or illusion. It is up to man to decide whether he will be man or beast.

In some illusions man seeks gardens and thrones of oneness with God...ignoring the fact that only they have caused this separation, ignoring the fact that God...your God...my God...would want man and woman...woman and man to exist in the garden together.

For I...man...now know that you are the key to my re-entry...and I am the key to yours.

Man will chose a religion...but cannot chose to love.

Man has stopped the folly of offering anything to God today. Man no longer can afford the luxury of marching virgins to the mouth of the volcano...man no longer has the time to slaughter sheep. For these efforts interfere with the Relig-a-thon phone lines that implore millions to send in their subscriptions...phone lines that implore millions to send for this book...that tape...that recording...that reading. The flock must buy- buy- buy and sell- sell- sell.

Man wants us to build him great churches, but in reality, of what value is a magnificent church when God originally gave us the most beautiful place of all to worship? For did not God give us planet earth?

And of what value are collected funds if they do not all go to the poor and the needy...and not to the rich and the greedy?

Men have purposely made the worship of God a complex and subjective activity. They revise and redo...redirect and misdirect...add to and leave out as historians attempt to fit God into their media slot.

History records numerous attempts to promote monotheism as far back as 1385 BC...as men looked to the Sun God in Egypt.

In Persia there was the religion of Zoroaster in 630-553 BC. He promoted one God...a prince of evil who opposed the prince of peace...a battle for good and evil...final judgement...immortality...rules to live by and the belief in a new world. Zoroaster preached that after death the soul passes either into heaven or hell... life through procreation...combating evil, and that human weakness may be forgiven and erased by confession or the transfer of merits from saints.

In 535 BC it was believed that the Buddha left home...reached enlightenment...believed in one God...the need for a personal savior...the power of prayer...eternal life in heaven or hell and life after death. Are not these stories of religious history similar in case after case...in religion after religion as man attempts to explain the unexplainable?

Have we not heard these stories before...will we not hear them again? Will man not always find new texts...new prophets...new Gods and new concepts of heaven or hell?

There are many versions of virgin births...
resurrections from the dead...ascensions to the
heavens...miracles of life and the belief that man will
ascend to the heavens for living a pious life starting
from the beginning of time.

Adonis from virgin mother Myrrh
Cyrus from virgin mother Mariana.
Hermes from virgin Maia
Joshua from virgin mother Miriam.
Buddha from virgin mother Maya.
Krishna from virgin mother Maritala
and Jesus from the virgin mother Mary.

The letter M has traveled with the virgin for thousand
of years.

Will ancient men with ancient minds not
continue to borrow beliefs as has been done from the
beginning of time?

Will ancient men with ancient minds not
continue to involve us in war after war...religion after
religion...God search after God search...modification
after modification...revision after revision of man's
basic beliefs in the concept of God?

God's word is not to be found in the
conflicting words of religious scripture...for the
language of God can not be recorded or deciphered...
unless it is done through the heart of an individual.

For even today one cannot translate the simplest form of poetry without perhaps totally losing its meanings from one language to another.

There is no "How to Book" to reach a God consciousness...for why would the God that can program us all need to write a book?

And if there were need for written scriptures... who would allow them to stand unadulterated...and what race would resist the urge to re-write them according to their customs or goals?

Would the Essenes in BC not have their version...and what would be found in the Apocrypha "Hidden Books of the Bible" that the church leaders decided should remain hidden from the world?

Would not the Jews, the Christians, the Church of Rome, writers translating from Aramaic to Hebrew to Greek to Latin then to English, alter most of its original concepts, as words, customs, interpretations, likes and dislikes, prejudices angers, hatreds and racisms all have different meanings?

And as they mix and match...and match and mix, all will say that *their* scripture is the word of God...and let no dog bark.

Would the book languish as a forgotten cloak on a rack...waiting to be adorned and claimed by anyone who reached out for its warmth...wrapping themselves in a cloak of insularity...refusing to offer its comfort to others?

For as men sat in council between the pagans or the church, they mutually agreed to accept one truth… and that was that the mistreatment and control of women was a God given right.

Ancient men with ancient minds moved on to more important matters, such as, was the earth flat...was hell in the center of the earth continually burning...and matters such as decisions concerning the burning of accumulated books of learning.

Ancient men with ancient minds discussed more important issues like who should be Pope...who should be Priest and who should be Bishop and how to control the minds of the masses.

Issues such as, who should receive lashes...how many and how hard...who should be beheaded...and who should be burned at the stake, all headed the concerns of the early religious orders...and all took priority over the rights and needs of women.

Yesteryears issues such as, should Israel fall to the Assyrians in 722 BCE or should Judah fall to the Babylonians in 587 BCE...should Jerusalem be destroyed...what temple or church to burn or sack and today the issues are where to transfer those in the church hierarchy that have been accused of child molestation... As leaders become co-conspirators...accessories after the fact...secretly allowing another flock to be abused by the wolves in sheep cloths.

How many caught...how many guilty?

Will you not research the concept that Christianity strayed from the Torah, the sacred religion of the Jews, and allowed women a somewhat better plight?

Will you not witness Constantine as he establishes a totalitarian state religion as a replacement for the old Roman state, in order to exercise its power over the masses?

Is it not written and plainly stated?

Will your search begin with the Christian churches need to establish its power and begin by claiming that all interpretations and stories in the Bible must come from those selected by powerful bishops in order to concentrate the power in the church?

Was any of this from the hand of God?

Did Peter and Paul, in opting to work with the power of the church, stray too far from the laws of Moses...hence they were rejected by the Orthodox Jews who would have nothing to do with the numerous revisions of the religious text? Is that why the Orthodox Jews will only accept the first five books of Moses and acknowledge Jesus of Nazareth as only a mere man?

Or would you search for understanding beginning with the declaration by the Roman Church that they must establish the monopoly on religious beliefs as "outside of the church there is no salvation."

Hence the church set about declaring all other believers and religions as heretics.

Or will your search begin with the premise that religion is not a matter of an individual's personnel communion with God or Christ, but it is merely the matter of whether an individual is willing to accept someone else's testimony of truth and believe it unquestionably? Or will your search begin with the Coptic Scriptures in Egypt or Syria...or will it begin with the lost chapters of the Bible which were authorized to be hidden from the eyes of man by the church?

Or do you even want to search or know the results of the deception of ancient men with ancient minds?

If not, please read no further and fall on your knees to ancient men with ancient minds...hoping that they will find the time to speak to God on your behalf between wardrobe changes and speech writing.

But if you...woman...begin your search, you will find that it is time to address the issues that affect your life...as man continues to war over the very subject that should unite the world...the search for God.

Man continues to war over interpretations of scriptures even today. And you will find that from the beginning of time man has spent thousands of years engaged in these senseless wars, sacrificing us all.

In your search will you be bold enough to question the four recorders of the gospels?

Would you find any truth to the theory that Mark wrote with the help of the notes of Andrew, since Mark was but a child at the time of Christ...and that he wrote as directed by Simon Peter, who was attempting to please the Church of Rome who wanted a documented written word of the teaching of Christ? Or that Mark wrote from his and Peter's memory over 40 years after the passing of Christ?

And would you not find it strange that Mary or Jesus of Nazareth would not document or produce one word of history, being blessed with a believed direct communications with God, who would know of the carnage caused by the conflict of religious interpretation?

And would you cling to the five beginning chapters of Genesis that the Jews would defend as only the word for their people, denying that there is a relevant message to any others...North...East...South... or West, affirming that Moses was only concerned for *his* people?

Did not the Africans deserve to find a promised land...did not the Orientals deserve to find a promised land...did not other enslaved people of the world deserve to be released from bondage?

Did God only speak to the issues of a chosen people, leaving the rest of the world to await their settlement before peace would come?

Would you allow anyone to limit the scope of God's hand? Would God not hear the cries of all?

Would God not know of the rich and the poor...
the high and the low...the white and the black...the red
and the yellow...the cultured and the uncultured...the
educated and the uneducated...the animalistic and the
spiritual...the religious and the unreligious...the moral
and the immoral?

And would God...your God...my God...our
God...not show concern for them all?

Would God not be concerned that you...woman...
were told to sit in silence in the church, accepting that
you were not allowed to speak as this would be deemed
a disgrace and that the church would be punished if it
allowed any woman to speak directly to God...your
God...my God...our God?

Would you question if there were any truth to the
fact of the appointment of 10 women, chosen by Jesus
of Nazareth, to serve as teachers and deaconesses to
spread the Christian word, and that this teaching of
women had been abandoned on his death...as Paul, the
Apostle, allowed the ancient customs to again place
woman in her place...far from the base of religious
freedom on the direction of the church?

And how would you view the concept of
ancient men with ancient minds who decreed that
women must cover their hair as it length and beauty was
an affront to God...the very God that had created this
mane of hair for you woman...any woman...all women.

And is there any truth that the Gospel of Matthew was written in Aramaic solely for the edification of the Jews…while having a ghost writer in the form of Isador write in Greek?

Did Isador write the book of Matthew in 71 AD. from the notes of Matthew?

Is Luke's Gospel really the gospel of Paul coupled with notes from Matthew and written in 82 AD? Has the Gospel of John, the son of Zebedee, been written and re-written to make it appear as if John was the author while he had his associate Nathan, a Greek from Caesarea, write from the memory of John?

And were all four gospels written by Matthew, Mark, Luke and John to awaken faith and belief in what *they* believed? Was it only *their*story drawn from memory some 40 to 80 years after the life of their savior? And were all four gospels written by Matthew, Mark, Luke and John commissioned and restructured by the Church of Rome?

And then where would we fit Tyndale's 16th century translations of the Bible, as he preferred English to Greek, Hebrew, Latin or German?

In Anglo-Saxon times even more of the Bible was lost in translation and was again altered to reflect the rulers thoughts and needs for control of the masses?

And then when Norman French was the dominant language between the 11th and 13th century, did Latin, which was the language of authority, cause English to again lapse?

And where do we place the story of the refugees in Geneva that in 1557 added the verses and then revised the whole Bible in 1560…or the revisions of Arch Bishop Parker in 1568…or Cloverdale with his great Bible in 1539?

Or what of King James IV of Scotland or the Bishop's Bible in 1572…or Protestant John Wesley in 1755…or Presbyterian scholar James Moffit in 1913… or the Anglican priest J.B. Phillips in 1958 in contemporary English…and the Good News Bible in 1976? All written by the hand of man as in the beginning.

And is it true that the Archbishop of Canterbury was the first to eventually designate chapters in the Bible in the 13th century…and should we add the historical account of James VI of Scotland who authorized 54 "learned" men to translate the Bible back into Greek and Hebrew and allowed "comments and observations" from the clergy as the work progressed?

Were these comments and observations by these 54 learned men also the word of God? And is it true that they had **license** to alter where necessary by "any learned man in the land"…be he good or bad…of faith or of no faith? Did it not matter what quality of man had license to alter?

And what of the fact that at one time all publishing rights rested in the crown of England and there rested the power to print whatever the church so decreed...and the domination of the masses through the power of forced persecution of those that did not believe as the rulers decreed?

Would this interference be the hand of God?

Would the findings of various religious scripts first be documented among the Greeks, who would also claim virgin births by the Gods...ascension to heaven by earthly men who would then become Gods with the ability to affect the life of man on earth...and beliefs that the Gods resided in the heavens and watched and affected the antics of humanity?

Would the Greeks be the first to claim vengeful Gods...breathing fire and brimstone, sending bolts of lightning and thunder to chastise their human creations long before the destruction of Sodom and Gomorrah.

Would the Greeks claim the six-sided hexagram star as their own, only to have it resurface as the Star of David? And would the Greeks take all of the credit for the concept that women were inferior to men, as decreed by Hesiod in the 8th century BC and repeated in later religious texts, because some of them found more pleasure in the arms of men and children...a practiced still found in the inner sanctums of various churches and religions yet today?

Religious scriptures have been rewritten...edited and revised for thousands of years. Were any of these the hand of God...your God...my God...our God?

Depending on their upbringing, most believe that what they were taught is the truth...and in their isolation...they believe that all foreigners believed in false Gods.

Man has coupled idolatry with paganism...and mysticism with voodooism. He has borrowed from one religion and sold out, one to the other, and does not know where his belief begins or ends. He has allowed pomp and circumstance to feed on the time of God...and he prepares the pulpit as in one act plays, taking titles of self evaluation designating themselves as "Your Grace... Your Eminence...Your Holiness…Reverend Father and Father" and other religious titles of ascendancy, voted... selected and elected to equalize with God. But it is reported that even Jesus of Nazareth said: "But all their works they do for to be seen by men: They make broad their phylacteries and enlarge the borders of their garments: Loving the uppermost rooms at feast, and the chief seats in the synagogues: But he that humbles himself shall be exalted."

Merry men, taking value in a secret society, playing at being God and explaining it all as a ceremony for God!

Imitation is the highest form of flattery, but there is no honor in imitating God, for this attempt at imitation will doom the world as self-appointed holy men fight for control of the masses. It is fit for a Broadway play as they slowly walk by...in flowing robes trimmed in gold, offering a hand to kiss here...a foot to kiss there...a ring to kiss, or the hem of their garment, and always the awaited valueless touch of blessings from ancient men with ancient minds.
Is no one struck by the comedy of it all?

They sit on thrones of plush cushioned velvet... hand carved by craftsmen out of the finest of materials, while we, the masses, sit on common cramped benches...sardine to sardine.

They, in their self appointed positions, represent a secret society and tell us to sing...to pray...to open our mouth...to drink...to bow our head...to confess...to walk...to stand...to sit...and to go and sin no more as they take on the role of God with an authority based on empty air.

They demand that one pay 10 % or more which equals 100% more than that requested by God.

Is no one struck by the comedy of it all?

Man has not realized that the gifts from God will never be available to man in this confusion.

While God sets one path for man...man has forged tributaries with no inlets leading to God.

But now we must seek this path to God together...untitled as "Your Grace...Your Holiness... Priest or King...moving forward as merely man and woman...and woman and man, for titled or not, we are all far from the path and getting farther.

Man says God is here...God is there. God is with us and against them. Man says our God will protect us while other men fall to their knees in the throes of death...wondering why their God failed them, all falling victims of faulty interpretations of God's design.

Men cry "God be with us..."as he destroys
men and women in war after war...men and brothers...
woman and sisters...all created by God, but yet all
destroyed in the name of God!

Man cannot get it right whether politics...love or
religion. These ancient concepts and interpretations have
led us to the brink of war, and beyond, on all continents.

When did we allow someone to pick our
God..your God or mine? When did we give up the right
to directly acknowledge God...the God of our
beginning...the God of our creation? When did we
acknowledge that someone, other than any of us, are the
chosen people of God...your God...my God...our God?

When did we allow *the concept of God* to be
separated from our personal experience?

When did we allow any religion to automatically
become *our* religion? Some religious orders, no more
than glorified cults, now having the command of armies,
staggering finances, and the ears of the world. Religious
orders built on the backs of the world's population...
while others declare that they are the chosen people...the
keeper of God's keys.

But yet today they incorporate the world,
seeking more flock to confuse...more conflict to spread.
Today they now claim that *the word* is universal and
meant for the world, as they re-edit and revise...realizing
that they are not threatened by the inclusions of others
as all religions attempt to control world opinion.

And they continue to manipulate.

On the world stage and at sumptuous summit dinners for heads of state, they wine and dine and posture and speak of peace...but in the wings they plan for the destruction of whole communities and design and implement ethnic cleansings...all for their concept of God compliance.

And we are all to blame...you and I...man and woman...woman and man, for we have not learned to decipher God for ourselves.

It is inconceivable that God...your God...my God...our God, would create humanity to join warring religious factions bent on destroying the world's population...including mothers and fathers...sisters and brothers...husbands and wives and all of the innocents of the world.

Factions that seek out innocent men and women...those easily led...ready fodder for those who have learned the power of control. Believers that do not know the questions...following those who do not have the answers.

Sheep like...a flock...led by whomever takes the lead... whether good shepherd or bad.

For I hear ancient man's prayer to Zeus when he asked, " O Zeus, why have you settled woman in the light of the sun...women...this bane mankind finds counterfeit?"

If you wished to propagate the human race, it was not from woman you should have given us this, rather, men should have put down in the temples either bronze or iron or a mass of gold and have brought offsprings, each man for a price corresponding to his means, and then dwelt in houses free from the female sex."

And I hear the voice of Apollo when he argues that "The mother is not parent to her child, but nurse only of the new-planted seed that grows; the parent is he who mounts."

"He who mounts."

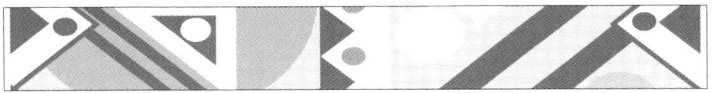

4
ARE YOU LOVED?

s it love if I love you today and another tomorrow? Is this not better labeled as lust...or desire? Lust demands immediate satisfaction while love must be nurtured and allowed to grow.

Lust, temptation and desire will allow one to shut out the one you profess to love...while love will never allow this exclusion.

Not loving lies at the core of our problems...and if love were a product sold in the market it would be worth any price. We are now paying the ultimate price for a loveless life...no refunds and no exchanges...no warranties and no guarantees...and this loveless love has no shelf life.

Should there be a school for love...can there be a school for love...for is it not obvious that we need to know more of this thing called love?

Do you love...are you loved...are you capable of loving or of being loved? I say yes...for you are the object of my love...and I wish to be the object of yours.

We must learn to love with the ability to control our self satisfaction...our desire for affectionate sexual possession and our lust...for this control is what separates us from the animals who are uncontrollable in their sexual expressions.

The intensity of love must be sustained in our minds, though expressed through our bodies...for when it is confined to the body we will never find peace...for the memory and the desire for this intensity will drive us to acts and crimes of passion.

We will never know the exact chemistry of love as too much will kill what we love and too little can cause us to lose what we love. Who decides when we love too much or too little...who knows when enough is enough...or less is more?

Regardless of this dilemma, our quest is to find love and sustain it to the satisfaction of each other, for if we are to prepare our future...learning to love is a must, for if not, we deny God's plan.

We must learn to love and to express our version of loving...and our version must be an act of love and not infatuation...for infatuation will disappear at the end of act one or even before it is completed.

Infatuation can be based on the car one drives or the clothes one wears. It can be blinded by the house one lives in or the job one has. It could be influenced by the finances or the name...or the talk...or the walk...or any number of superficial, valueless articles in one's possession.

One's infatuation and the reasons for this infatuation cannot stand the course of examination or of close scrutiny, but love…true love…has no faults and can truly withstand the test of time.

Mature love needs little to rekindle the fire…as memories of love remains…burning in our loins.

Love is too complex an emotion to define as is the interpretation of beauty…for love is controlled and housed in an unfathomable area of human emotion.

Love cannot be categorized and even though poets attempt to describe the emotions of love…they touch but a corner of the love that man and woman are capable of.

It is obvious that the inhabitants of this world, as we know it, are more easily persuaded to accept the sharing of the emotions of hate, fear and intolerance as these emotions appear to spark neighbors more easily than the emotion of love.

We now hate on a global scale that the world has never known as we nurture our hate through the miracles of modern media. Hate of neighbors comes through the lens of hand held cameras thousands of miles away, or from satellite dishes which hovers over the heads of all the world…exchanging messages of misunderstanding and misinformation…of brutality and intolerance, allowing our children and all future generations to see man's inhumanity to all…
showing mirror images of man's inhumanity to humankind.

Interpretations of these visual global images come through the mouths of public officials, leaders of government, speech writers, politicians, military commanders and the media, and benefit business leaders who tell us enough to stir our emotions in the direction that will allow them to maintain their financial objectives.

Again ancient men with ancient minds retard the emotions of love while nurturing emotions that will serve their purposes.

Ancient men with ancient minds will redefine God's plan and will attempt to convince their legions that they and they alone have the answer to the problems of the world, even as these problems worsen before our unbelieving eyes.

Weapons of mass destruction will now begin to fall on the heads of those who had only experienced the effects of nature coming from above. The innocent, who have always been the major victims of war and religious conflicts, will continue to pay the price.

Moslems against Christians...Christians against Moslems...Jews against Arabs...Arabs against Jews... Jews against Muslims...Muslims against Jews and all against the concept of a one true loving God.

Have we not seen this war among religions before? Have we not seen the images of the innocent lying in limp postures, shedding the same color blood that we all possess?

Have we not seen enough death, destruction and mayhem in small villages where the helpless attempt to shield their small children from the tons of raining steel that find them wherever they knell?

Have we not seen enough schools and churches blown to bits by weapons of mass destruction manned by young soldiers that knew not why they released the weapons of destruction on those below?

Can love rain down so easily?

For love is all that we must seek while here on earth, for seeking and knowing its value distinguishes us from the animals. Animals can mourn, hurt, protect love ones, think, and plan. They can emulate many of man's acts and emotions. But only humans seeks and performs acts of love in hopes that they are deciphering the will of the creator.

We will acknowledge this difference and in our home of love, we will give the greatest gift of all...the gift of one's self to the other.

For when we give of ourselves there is no material gift that can surpass, for the question becomes, can we love God but yet not love the creations made by God? Creations which are you and I...man and woman...woman and man.

For I hear ancient man's prayer to Zeus when he asked, " O Zeus, Why have you settled woman in the light of the sun, women, this bane mankind finds counterfeit? If you wished to propagate the human race, it was not from woman you should have given us this, rather, men should have put down in the temples either bronze or iron or a mass of gold and have brought offspring's, each man for a price corresponding to his means, and then dwelt in houses free from the female sex."

And I hear the voice of Apollo when he argues that "the mother is not parent to her child, but nurse only of the new-planted seed that grows; the parent is he who mounts."

Ancient men with ancient minds influence the church of today that still deny your role on this earth and continues to echo these prayers and arguments yet today. And as man defines the essence of God…and the image of God…does he also attach a male appendage to God, as man believes that he and God bear the same image?

Once you were the spoils of war…but now you must spoil the war, for you supply the fodder for the battlefield as your sons fight the battles lost by their fathers…and fathers fought battles lost by their fathers and ancient men with ancient minds sanctioned their wars of religion years before they sanctioned love for you.

I pause to ask that you forgive my rambling journey back and forth...forth and back...as I know not where to begin to break this chain of ignorance that binds us both. Do I begin in the past...to be beaten and bogged down in history...or do I begin today and be accused of disrespect and religious infidelity?

Dare I attempt to awaken you from your sleep either self-induced or induced by those that love you not...or do I leave you to sleep away your days while taking your need for love to the grave...condemning your children to follow your path?

By my request to examine your past and witness the placing of the yoke around your neck...do I commit an injustice? And when the blame is laid will you find a supplement to fill this void now that the truth is known, or have I committed an equal wrong by attempting to replace controlled religion with a personal religion with God, a relationship not dictated by ancient men with ancient minds.

Should I tip-toe into the woman's chambers of ignorance...selecting only this one or that one to accompany me on my journey...evaluating your need to walk with man while leaving some to sleep, and some to dream and some to continue the nightmare of a loveless relationship, never knowing the love promised by God?

Once you are awakened from your sleep...will you not call out to your sons and daughters, freeing them from their sleep of the dead...sleeping so deeply and so soundly that they would sleep past the call for love and respect, and would continue to live as dictated by ancient men with ancient minds.

Men that would not allow them freedom from the miniature chains that will surely grow if they do not learn how to love before they learn how to obey.

For the need to love is the basis for our existence...only distracted by the manipulations of those seeking the throne of God.

For prayer without love is useless...as is the repetitive repeating of meaningless phrases in an attempt to program the mind that this is what God demands. We must teach our young the value of love and then teach them how to transfer that love around the world on the wings of personal prayer. For prayer is the vehicle for the transportation of love from man to God...from woman to God...from man to woman...and from woman to man. This concept of love is what should be repeated over and over, not cultural scriptures written by ancient men with ancient minds.

Who will teach us to recognize the emotions of our hearts as we seek each other? Who will teach us the value of our touch and it's healing powers? Must I ignore the gentleness of your touch that can heal me as no medicine can, even when my mind and my body have yet to diagnose my illness? Does my respect and admiration of your attributes weaken me so that I fall physical victim to other men that love and respect you not? Can a self appointed holy man supply me with the emotion of a loved mate?

I think not...for our love and the need for that love will give us the strength of which even Samson would have envied.

Will adherence to your words of wisdom place me at some disadvantage...and will my feelings of love for you and the desire to be in your company make others who are void of woman superior in their judgement of life?

And what sign will my forehead bear for taking strengths from both mother and father...never separating their value...never choosing one over the other...never loving one less or one more...when they gave equally, as able?

But for now, I must replace this anger at ancient men with ancient minds as it distracts from my goal here today...to seek your understanding of my understanding. To seek to find our love...to find our respect...to find our passion for each other and to seek the approval of your God...my God...our God...as we seek to communicate our needs to each other.

When we walk together as man and woman... woman and man...we must be able to now recognize man's deformed structures. Structures that have been presented to us as divine structures, passed as the word of God by ancient men with ancient minds, passed by men who will attempt continuously to make their heaven here on earth, while creating a hell for us all.

And though I lack the eloquence of words and their proper structure...I ask you to edit my construction in your hearts...and not in a school of grammar...for if you come with me you will feel the power of my love for you...woman...any woman...all women...and proper words and proper grammar will not be necessary.

For I do not have time to rhyme or select words to make them sing...I do not have thoughts of musical words...nor a desire to be compared with poets of the past.

This will not bear the frivolity of the Song of Solomon...as his song were sung into the wombs of hundreds of women...but yet he was honored among ancient men with ancient minds as an honorable role model.

For I view our task as more important than these trivial pursuits...for what are words that rhyme but make no sense...and what are words that attempt to sing, but lack the music of love...and what are poets without man and woman...woman and man?

For without love we will continuously make noises to God...but they will not be joyous.

For man can no longer exist as a stranger to you woman...any woman...all women...and so I will offer these passages as an apology to you...woman...all woman...any woman, in hopes that you, who are seeking to understand the reason for your burden, will begin this journey back into the teachings of ancient man...hoping to find where God's plan changed to that of man's.

Hoping that upon your return...we will together begin our original journey...side by side according to the will of our creator.

For today's challenges have changed for us both...as you are no longer measured by your ability to bear man many sons...nor crush his grapes...nor make his wine...nor make his bread...nor suffer in silence.

No longer must rulings be made in your absence by angry men that professed to hear the word of God in isolated mountain caves directing them to continue to make war and continue to exclude you from your rightful place in the world.

For all things have their season, and if you do not feel that your season...together with man as an equal...has come...then you should prepare your winter shroud...as your life will continue to be a winter of discontent.

Have you accepted the history of man...with his history of misinformation? Have you accepted the hand of man with his willingness to tamper with the will of God? Have you accepted that there could be a word of God not available to you?

I ask that you woman...any woman...all women...give our world another chance. It is not time to re-write *his*tory but to write *our*story. For I have taken no pleasure in my findings for they have shamed me and enslaved me and they have caused me pain.

And if you do not feel the indignation of the injustices to you...woman...any woman...all women, then I will move on...seeking a more indignant mind, for I cannot believe that woman...any woman...all women...will accept the findings of her past.

5
PLAYING GOD

nd now...today...I have the sense no...the desire to survive...to step forward to you uncertain as to how I will be received by you...uncertain as to whether the time is now or never. For by now we both should have seen the error of our ways. Errors by you and I...man and woman...woman and man.

We now must make a new choice as to whom we love and how we love. It must not be bound by religion, for God gave no choices as to what religion to follow...to live by..to love by...or to die by. Man made this selection from his limited vision...and is ready to kill to enforce it.

Man has created these multiple religions...these multiple Gods...these multiple options...these multiple laws and rules concerning our relationship and our worship with God.

In his folly, man attempts to give a name to God...and a place for God...and a special people for God to protect, but never a special race other than the one that they belong. And they implore of God to protect them in battle and to help them destroy the enemy who is their brother...sister and children of God!

And this has created the problem.

These interpreters of God's will are old fashioned and self-serving. They attempt to interpret God's will for their benefit and our damnation.

They cite ancient writers as selectors of the prophets of God as we would select a coat to wear, based merely on our frame of mind. They cite ancient writers as selectors of God. They site ancient writers as the selectors of mysteries that could not be revealed to mere man ever. In today's court they would have been found guilty of fraud in the most elementary court of law. Ancient men long since dead and gone...long since proven wrong…long since suffering from wanting to be God.

These same ancient men said that the world was flat…that the sun revolved around the earth …that burning bushes could talk and that life came from dust. Were they not wrong? But yet these same ancient men from ancient times...are the guidelines accepted by man to control you and to control me and to explain God to us all.

Man alters any ancient law to serve his benefit and man will alter any modern law to serve his benefit. Be he king or Pope...be he powerful or wealthy...be he cunning or knowledgeable. Man will alter man for his benefit...and man will alter God for the same end. How convenient as they make the laws for the enslavement of the races…and say that it is the will of God.

They destroy the religions of others and say that it was *their* God's will. They enslaved the masses and said that God directed them to.

They have caused religious war after religious war and entered into battle with the cry of "In the name of God," while slaughtering God's creation by the millions.

We have allowed them to play at being God for so long that they now feel that it is their right...and in playing God, they defy God's vessel of life...woman...of which you are. It is as if they would defy God's selection of you as the mother of life.

They disrespect your womb and the results of intercourse with that chamber with a passion that they are willing to die for or kill for, but yet will kill to possess that very same chamber. Religious control... legal control...social control and political control... they must have all. They beat their chests and pass laws forbidding acknowledgement of your rights and purpose here on earth. And this ancient interpretation of the will of God by men of all races...of all countries...of all religions, is where we must begin...as in the beginning.

We are in a maze...not sure of where we are... not sure of where we began, and not sure of where we are going. But I would rather be lost with you than on a sure path by myself. For together we can produce life... even in this maze.

In their desire to claim God like status they continue to take titles of reverence and designate titles to themselves, seeking to out do others with the same title as they elevate from "Reverend to Very Reverend...to Right Reverend to Most Reverend"...all seeking to be as revered as God...with titles to imply some separation from man.

Titles not given by God...but titles taken and awarded by man to man…a secret society...the ayes have it.

These titles awarded for the sole purpose of playing God. Seeking these titles have caused wars and destruction as they fight for turf with pomp and circumstances…ceremony and performance… pageantry and theatre...paganism and idolatry.

Where as God's creation of woman was a helpmate to the humanity of man…ancient man saw women as property...as slaves…as second-class citizens, not capable of teaching…leading…or administrating to our future, solely on earth for the purpose of playing the role designated by ancient men with ancient minds.

How arrogant!

Woman…qualified to birth man…raise man... teach man…nurse man…cure man…soothe man...feed man...comfort man…love man…and bury man…but never allowed to share equal status with man once man is up and about.

Man…then passes laws which would shame God...if God were capable of this emotion...relegating woman to the status of personal property or less.

Woman...a creature to be tolerated…humored... tricked...scorned...admonished…discarded...traded... sold...beaten and blamed for the evils of the world. A soul to be humiliated…deceived…and forced to bear false witness to the superiority of man.

Remove your veil, or your Burqa, for God did not decree this guise...man did.

For the veil that men wear is invisible, but yet blocks their total view of life as God planned it.

Thrown out of an imaginary garden, man looked back in anger and imagined that he saw you, woman, as the reason for this ejection...as the cause for the separation from God.

If we are to start anew we must begin at the beginning...at the gates of a new garden...at the gates of the division...at the gates of the laying of blame by ancient men with ancient minds...at the gates of the misinterpretation of God's will.

We must walk together...not you behind and man in front...for our new challenges must be seen together. Our new challenges are now the challenges of compatibility...interpretation of the future and planning for this destiny. For when we come together...all things will become clear.

For this is how we originally left the concept of the first Garden. For this was when religion began, as man attempted to beg back, as man attempted to atone...as man sought the explanation of his rejection.

Man traveled North...South...East and West... and wherever he settled...he created his explanation of the reason for his exodus from the garden.

And in every direction...man languished...he pondered and he blamed woman. He blamed her for his imagined expulsion and his imagined separation from his God, he then created a religious indictment against woman.

Man then created religion...not knowing or caring that earlier man had already cast blame on you as the cause of all evils.

A religion in the North...a religion in the South...a religion in the East and a religion in the West, all professing that the way to God was through them...all professing that they knew the Son of God... are the Son of God or knew who would be. And all professing that you...woman...were the cause for man's fall from grace.

And in their distant lands they took a vow which traveled throughout the world...linking them on one issue and one issue only...that you woman were to be ruled by them...man...all man...any man.

They believed themselves different in all other aspects...but united on the issue of women's place behind the throne or under the foot...convinced that God had permitted them to forever seek vengeance and control over you…woman...any woman...all women.

Ancient scribes attribute the treatment of woman to the rulings of God...as they descended from isolation from caves, mountain tops, deserts and from other places of isolation...all isolated and void of the love of woman...any woman...all women.

Always bearing their hallucinary findings with stone tablets or scrolls or some other ancient documents found and formed in places of isolation...void of the smell, feel or love of woman... and certainly void of the of the essence of God.

Isn't it time for this foolishness to stop?

But historical speculation reveals that prehistoric man exhibited the same orientation towards woman millions of years before...but he had the decency to refrain from attributing this ill treatment to the will of God. Prehistoric man wanted woman for release and insertion at his beck and call. Prehistoric man cared not for the emotion of woman...she was his to do as he saw fit...be it servitude...rape...or violence.

Are many of us any better today?

The treatment of woman is a man made act... written into the scriptures by men that fear God not at all. Men that exhibit qualities of non-believers, unmindful that they play at God and attribute edicts that could not have come from God, but they care not for this deception for they fear not God's wrath, if it exist.
Have you forgiven this deception...have you abandoned the need to better understand your plight... are you convinced that "thy will be done"...and that *will* is the yoke around your neck? Have you accepted the history of man with his history of misinformation? Have you accepted the hand of man with his willingness to tamper with the will of God? Have you accepted that there could be a word of God not available to you?

You were created inferior in physical strength, but yet ancient men with ancient minds still feared your power and denied you direct communication with your God...my God...our God.

I still would ask that you...woman...any woman...all women...give our world another chance.

It is not time to re-write *his-story* for it has been distorted beyond repair and we must spend our time writing *our*-story...man and woman...woman and man.

I have taken no pleasure in my findings...for they have shamed me and enslaved me...and they have caused me pain. And if you do not feel the indignation of the injustices to you...woman...any woman...all women...then I will move on...seeking a more indignant mind, for I cannot believe that woman...any woman...all women...will accept the findings of her past.

And as the numbers of incarceration of confused men and women increase...this estrangement is at the base of our problems. This estrangement that has caused the incarceration of men and women as they continue to be confused as to the value of men to women and women to men.

This estrangement caused by ancient men with ancient minds that did not allow us to discover the need for each other.

This estrangement that caused our men and women to lash out at each other rather than reach out for each other, fostered by believing the teachings of ancient men with ancient minds.

And if you do not feel the indignation of the injustices to you, then I will move on...seeking a more indignant mind, for I cannot believe that woman...any woman...all women...would accept the findings of their past, for unless you begin to think...you will return to the findings of ancient men with ancient minds and you will again misunderstand the will of God, while claiming that you are born again.

For we must leave ancient men with ancient minds to argue among themselves as we walk by hand in hand as God planned.

For the ancient rulings that they now cling to is but a record of man's personal interpretation of history, and they will only be revisiting the pages of history that originally caused the conflict in a never ending cycle of ignorance. For as they seek religion, they only establish a personal method of religious attitude and social practices which reflect the history or culture of a particular region, nation or race.

But yet ancient man sat in a self imposed incarceration and attempted to read and study manufactured theology in an attempt to interpret his role here on earth.

Man's study of ancient man-made scriptures will not set him free to know God.

In what ancient scriptures does God give the right of might to destroy whole races...while using the battle cry of "In the name of God?"

Is life just a game created by God...with God as the sole spectator...pitting man against man...race against race...religion against religion and man against woman?

Did God give the world multiple religious views and then sit back and watch the world destroy itself fighting to be the dominant religion?

Is this the first game created by God for the new world?

6
THE EAR OF GOD

oday...our love...or lack of love...is once more illuminated...visible...uncovered. Can it now be brought alive as intended... can it show that it can withstand the years of abuse...able to forgive and forget?

Can it forget the holocaust of the past...of old abuses and the subconscious effect of these abuses? Those abuses, so buried and so confusing that no rational explanation of their cause and effect can be found.

Enough of ancient laws for modern women... enough of ancient laws by ancient men...enough of ancient laws for a modern world...for ancient man has brought ancient solutions to this world and they reek of staleness and decay...hence the wars continue...void of love and respect...void of the sweetness of life... willing to make God a co-conspirator in their interpretation of the role of woman and man...man and woman.

Economic wars can be settled...wars among neighbors can be settled...but the pilot light of religious wars can burst into flames of hatred at the slightest breeze and can then burn forever.

Wars that cannot be resolved, as self appointed holy men dressed in the black robed garbs of death or flowing white robes with gold trim or shiny double breasted suits of charlatans with coiffured hair and massive media time, seek to maintain their roles as interpreters of God's designs.

But we...you and I...man and woman...woman and man...must together find our new love. To begin again we must steel ourselves from the onslaught of ridicule, as these imposters will spare no effort in attempting to maintain the shackles of our ignorance.

For their role is not defined in the real order of God, for they have self imposed their role contrary to God's wishes. They have magnified their role by continued conflicting interpretation of ancient scriptures and have compounded their confused thoughts for hundreds, no, thousands of years, while religious wars cover the globe and people die for religious causes that God never imagined would cause their deaths.

And all for the common good...their common good...as they now chart a new path for your communication with God, now claiming that it was written that the road to God lies through them and their teachings, while knowing that they will never be collectively blamed or indicted for their complicity in defining these false paths.

My path to God is not to be found through ancient robed men waving pagan instruments of smoke and shamelessly distributing artificial symbols of my Gods body. For my God's blood does not flow from wholesale products for my God is already within me.

They will use the miracles of life's mysteries to hold you in awe of what occurs everyday somewhere in this world as documented by "Ripley's Believe It or Not."

Ripley's "Believe It or Not" contains more unexplained miracles than all of the worlds ancient scriptures combined.

Miracles of returning to life after being pronounced dead...miracles of the restoration of sight miracles of inhuman displays of strength...miracles of kindness and love and forgiveness...which are true miracles.

Miracles found everyday in hospitals...on battlefields and in areas of nature's ravages. Miracles found and noted in the media throughout the world even today.

Unexplained miracles that the ancient imposters cite to prove their false interpretations of the mysteries of the past...attempting to hold you in their grasp just a few more thousand years.

And as they fool the world...the world becomes more foolish...and as they fool the world...this imperfect world becomes more foolish and more imperfect.

For they attempt to convince us that it is the opposition to the God of their choice that is the problem...when in reality...the problem is their opposition to God.

For did not God…with all wisdom…create a direct link? Is not the communication link with God within us all?

Why do they attempt to foster the written words of a mere mortals on the world as words of God?

I repeat…why do they attempt to foster the written words of a mere mortals on the world as the word of God?

Every religion has recorded the imaginary or perceived words or deeds of their God… but yet by force of arms these perceived words were declared null and void by another. By force of arms and by the might of man, not by the will of God, the people were put to death by invading armies…who allowed them life if they would renounce their chosen God for a foreign God…or death if they did not.

In all ancient scriptures they state that God give them the right of might to destroy whole races, while using the battle cry of —In the name of God.

Is life just a game created by God…with God as the sole spectator…pitting man against man…religion against religion? Did God give the world multiple religious views and then sit back and watch the world destroy itself fighting to be the dominant religion? Is this the first game created for the new world?

Did God create the new players for this game…deserving to be called "Father…Reverend Father…Most Reverend Father…Your Holiness…or Your Grace. Names that imply that they are the next best thing to God and are different from you and I.

In this game did God direct that man was to seek out the Pope...or the Bishop...or the Mullah or the Priest in order to communicate with God...or did man?

And these ancient men with ancient minds appear at our doorsteps as uninvited babysitters...and we...the children of God...are now the children of man...and we are treated as children.

Would God create such a self destructive game as the war of religions? Would God create the world to be decimated by man's interpretation of the will of God?

Man, in his isolation, was puzzled by his place on this planet and sought answers for his questions of "Why me?" But man was never able to escape the desires of the body, even though some sat in cold dark monasteries or mountain caves, hoping that the isolation would free the mind of the slavery of the body and they sought answers to the mysterious of the world...not in the light of the sun but in the cold darkness of caves or on mountain tops...all void of woman.

But even in these places the spirit of woman would not give his flesh any peace.

****

It was a day when Utheus decided that he would find the place and meaning of God, for he could stand the mystery no longer. He would today or tomorrow find the home of God...for it must be at the top of that mountain as predicted by the old ones who knew such things.

He would find God and speak to him and he would have revealed to him all of the secrets of heaven and hell...life and death...creation and the coming destruction of the world.

He had a right to know as he was obviously superior to woman and heathens who were forbidden to know the will of God. This he had been taught all of his life by the church elders, for had they not even forbidden woman from speaking in church or baring her hair? He would climb the mountain without food or drink as the divine one would surely supply his needs. As he ascended to the top he was surprised that the trip was so short and that he was there at the summit in no time.

He looked down on the world...for surely this mountain was the home of God. Since God would not sit on a small mountain and this was the tallest that he had seen in his region, which was the only region that he had ever seen, he was positive that he had found the home of God. He could see the horizon and since the world was flat, according to his elders, he knew that there was nothing else out there.

As the sun dropped off of the flat side of the earth he selected a spot on the ground facing East, as he had been taught that God would only receive his prayers if he prayed in that direction, in spite of the fact that God had also played no small part in creating the North, South and West.

It would just be a matter of time before God revealed himself and poured forth the answers to all of his questions. As the night chill set in he began to regret that he had not brought warmer clothing and a fire. He huddled closer to the large rock hoping that there was still some warmth in it from the earlier heat of the sun, and sitting on his haunches, he rested his chin on his chest and folded his arms below them.

He heard a sound coming from a distance to his left and he sat upright. Realizing that he should not present himself to the Most Holy One in a sitting position he quickly stood up. The dark brown lizard dragging a tail twice its size scurried past his feet and disappeared behind a rock. He slumped back to the ground and felt the cold further penetrate his body and so he curled into a fetal position and awaited the return of God.

As his head again dropped to his chest in an effort to diminish the chill in his bones, he imagined what he would do with the information given to him concerning the mysteries of God.

He could start a church with many followers who would sit at his feet and listen to his every word. Or, he could have an enormous temple built in his honor and sit on a throne forever and be served by virgin girls.

As thoughts of the virgin girls began to dominate his thoughts he began to think of the warmth of their bodies and how he wished that he had one to take his mind off the cold. His thoughts seemed to supply some real warmth and he began to fantasize that if he had one, or even two virgins, he would be able to wait a little longer for his enlightenment.

God it was cold. Maybe this was not the best time to come to be enlightened...maybe he should go and come back early in the morning so that he would at lest have the whole day to wait.

As he began his climb back down the mountain side he began to think of all the wasted time and effort he had just expanded climbing up and down this hill.

What explanation would he give to his friends when he told them that he had no messages from God and that he still did not know the source of life, or even the destination after death?

He would have thought that since he was superior to woman, that God would have made this information readily available to him since he was man and was told he was made in the image of God.

Well, he knew he would try again...but for now he would just tell them that women and the thought of women were incompatible with those seeking God, and that if you wanted the wisdom from the creator, all thoughts of women must be put out of your mind.

"I would have probably found God sooner if it had not been for the interference of the thoughts of woman. The next time I come to seek God I will put all thoughts of woman out of my head... for women are truly the downfall of man"

****

Again, a story ready for inclusion...ready for verse...ready for chapter...ready to be offered as proof of the wickedness of woman. Guilty without trial…guilty without jury...guilty without representation. Again, the ignorance of man...in his most primitive state...had completed the indictment of you...woman...any woman...all women. But yet we digest hundreds and thousands of stories such as these, with misunderstood and mistaken misinterpreted histories of wars with retributions...vengeance...punishments...violence and fear, preached from thousands of pulpits...temples and mosques around the world.

Reminders only of man's inhumanity to woman and man...void of the love of God.

Stories of constant incest...rape...violence...and anger. Sermons built on these subjects invoked the fear of God while God has asked that we invoke displays of love.

More stories of hate and revenge than sermons of love...more stories of man's inhumanity to man and woman than stories of man's need for the love of woman...or of woman's need for the love of man.

We must listen to the sermons...and we must decide. Do they hold out hope for the love of man and woman...woman and man..or do they preach ancient histories of ancient man from the perspective of an ancient limited few?

For these few have selected prophets that claimed to have heard the voice of their God...these few have selected those not qualified to hear the voice of their God...these few have selected those that are not to be included in the blessings of their God...these few have selected the continued wars that must continue in the name of their prophet and their God, and these few have selected the conflicts that plague the world today.

Why would God not make religious belief as free as the air we breath....or as clear as the waters of Antigua...so that all who stand on the shores can clearly see what lies beyond the surface?

PART II

LOST LOVE

We have not even been taught love...honor or respect, or even who were our heroes. For we have not even taught the stories of the first heroes. For this hero was not the first man to slay the dragon...nor was it David who slew Goliath.nor was it the first soldier to capture an enemy...nor was it the the first man that walked on the moon. For what would have been their heroic deeds without the hero of woman and the miracle of birth?

And as the archives list the names of great heroes where is the name of woman...any woman...all women?

7
A MATCH MADE BY GOD

here does your love hide when you do acts contrary to the act of loving? Does love resolve to solitary deep seated hate...directed towards just one man...or does it escape to the sea...filling every tributary with anger and desires of revenge towards all men...just waiting to overflow and drown the perpetrators of these age old injustices?

If love hides, was it ever an act of love...or have we never known true love? And where does man hide his love and respect for women...while doing acts of terror and violence?

For it is obvious that man relegates all love and respect for woman to some foreign chamber of his brain while committing these random acts of terrorism on the source of his continued existence...unmindful of the harm done to the future of humankind.

Can true love die or is it murdered? Is there a warning when love dies...or do we just distance ourselves and manufacture reasons and causes as we retreat to our solitary cave?

When we love, we use our bodies...our hearts and our minds as communicators. Our love is shown by respect and the willingness to give all, content to serve and to share, for above all...love is the gift of one's self to another.

But when we hate...these same components combine to create one of mankind's most destructive forces on earth. This same hate, when mixed with a feeling of misunderstanding, fear, rejection, violence and abandonment, becomes a substance that would put chemical warfare to shame.

This chemical of hate flows from woman to man...from man to woman...from man to man...from woman to woman...from woman to child...from man to child...from child to brother...from brother to sister...to friend and neighbor...and multiplies its strength upon its return to the originator...and then spews forth again and again with a greater resolve to continue to hate as it re-cycles this destructive emotion.

For we hate because we have not been taught who to love...how to love...or to love at all. For love has not been taught as emphasis was placed on ancient man's call for obedience.

We have not even been taught love...honor or respect, or even who were our heroes. For we have not even taught the stories of the first heroes. For this hero was not the first man to slay the dragon...nor was it David who slew Goliath...nor was it the first soldier to capture an enemy...nor was it the the first man that walked on the moon. For what would have been their heroic deeds without the hero of woman and the miracle of birth?

And as the archives list the names of great heroes where is the name of woman...any woman...all women?

And when they list the names of super heroes...why does not woman head this list?

Was the first hero in uniform...or was the first hero one who climbed into the fire to save a life? If that is the case then the first hero is woman...as she is clothed in the uniform of her sexuality and walks through the fire created by man's hostility.

But again you will find the scepter of the Greeks...as they define a hero as an illustrious man...a man descended from a God! Again confusion and illusion...again the conflict of myth and reality...again history contaminated with fictional myths and legends that reigns as the greatest hoaxes on the face of the earth, and continues to engulf our world.

For we must teach that the miracle of birth is the first act of heroism...as the first act of sacrifice...as the first act of God...your God...my God...our God... and we must teach the value of man and woman...and woman and man.

While Hero was the name in Greek mythology given to a Priestess of Aphrodite, a child's first hero must be the mother of their birth...that the child's first hero is the one allowing their body to be the chamber of life...while jeopardizing their own...for is this not what heroes do? The celebration of a newborn must be shared equally with the giver of that life, for if a taker of life is due a 21 gun salute in the name of war, then the salute given to woman must deafen the heavens, for birth is an act decreed by God...while the taking of life is an act against the wishes of your God...my God...our God.

****

And as the child suckled at her breast, she felt the heaving of his chest and gentle placed her fingers above the heart, closing her eyes and counting the rapid beats. The pain of the delivery had all but been forgotten and the screams of pain were now but an occasional cause for a moan as she gazed upon the results of this traumatic experience.

Upon waking, the nurse allowed her to hold her new born child and she could feel the emptiness in her body where the child had laid for nine months. The cavity was empty now, but yet it was a constant reminder of the child that had recently lay curled inside. As the nourishment flowed to her now swollen breast, she gentle pressed it closer to the small child's searching mouth, insuring that no air would pass onto his mouth.

She caught the whiff of his tobacco first, but did not immediately look up. She remembered his presence on many occasions as he entered her room during the last days of her pregnancy and while she feigned sleep she was aware that he was there standing over her looking at her swollen belly.

At the news of her announcement of her pregnancy, he had clutched her to him with such passion that she had almost fainted with the overwhelming feeling of his love for her. But she had then seen the confusion of his gaze as it fell on the suckling child...greedily nursing on the swollen nipple as the child's sound effects of its pleasure were broadcast throughout the room. She remembered how pale his face had become on that first day which gradually changed to one of displeasure.

Acknowledging the shadow beside the bed, she gazed upward into the stern face of her husband.

She would again recall this scene in the days and years to come and know that it was the beginning of their estrangement. She would recall his mounting anger at the sounds made by the child during the early days of breastfeeding. He would rage at her at the slightest provocation and she would eventually hide this act from him as often as possible. She noticed that he would not touch her breast as often as he had before her pregnancy and she was puzzled about what she had done to bring about this change in him.

She would eventually realize that at the point of the child's delivery, she was no longer a hero to her husband and that he would never again express his pleasure to her for her act of bravery and heroism. For the act of birth was now a thing of the past. The birth of the child would be separated from the act of giving birth, and the miracle of the birth would not be acknowledged ever again.

The child had claimed two areas of his wife's body that had been the sole domain and source of his pleasure...and he was not prepared for his reaction to this challenge. He was not prepared for the celebration of life coupled with the loss of his exclusive rights... and he was confused.

****

We have not reconciled the union of you and I...man and woman...and woman and man...and obviously we have not reconciled the heroes and heroines in our life. We have not reconciled the miracle of birth...and we have not reconciled the connection to God.

These subjects still confuse us today and will continue tomorrow unless we walk together with a new understanding of our presence here on earth. Free of the confusing past of our misinformation...free of ancient men with ancient minds...for we are strangers and are becoming more estranged by the minute.

Who will stop this cycle...who can stop this cycle...and how will we stop this cycle ?

We must withdraw from our self-built womb of protection of our feelings. We must speak touch and love. We must forgive for a moment the amount of injustice that we have known...you and I...man and woman...woman and man. We must not forget... allowing it to creep upon us again in another guise, but we must forgive the injustices of love...ignorance... race...and of war.

We must exchange our love willingly, while we forgive our damning past, for when we love we will not be party to those who do not, and by loving intensely, we will be showing the way to the rest of the world. For of all the pleasures that we might share with the world, what would be greater than to share the act of love?

One day we will be lovers…we must be…or we all will surely perish! We will be lovers…a match...as my God…your God…our God intended us to be.

We must learn to co-exist…for we are not each other's enemy, as ignorance of each other must bear that blame. The arguments that define this great gulf of differences between us are as needless and baseless as they are endless. I love you and I need to love you…for you are truly the only vessel for the world's continued life.

I share your pain, and having studied the basis of your pain, I wish to make amends as best I can, for had I not heeded your cry for help...I would never have heeded mine, as I was only a man and incomplete without you. Had I not been able to study and trace the patterns of your abuse by ancient men ...with ancient minds...I too would have magnified the differences between us...you and I...man and woman...woman and man.

We have tried the alternatives to love…group love…self love…commercial love…love-hate and no love at all. It is time to rethink these alternatives and accept the one true love…you and I…man and woman… woman and man.

So now we must sit in silence...wrapped in the protection of our needs...silently contemplating the wisdom of God in making us a match...content to escape from the anger of ancient men with ancient minds...who preach of vengeance from ancient scriptures...frightening the souls of man as he prostrates himself to these interpretations of the will of God.

For in these prone positions man cannot see his real oppressor...man cannot see the deception...man cannot see the attempts by man...to play God. But yet today I wonder, who has allowed these absurdities in religious garb to gain control of our world? Religious garb draped as costumes...costumes to deceive you and I...man and woman...woman and man.

Some men can never love...for they have locked this emotion away...and have bound their hearts with chains of unknown metals...with chains without locks... with chains without keys. They have locked themselves into dungeons without doors...dungeons without windows and dungeons without woman. They have allowed ancient interpretations to build prisons in their minds and foolishly attempt to search for the meaning of life without the guidance or the love of you...woman... any woman...all women.

But if you continue as a prisoner, then the road of recovery is made that much harder, for it would be unjust of me to implore you to free your mind of the teachings of ancient men with ancient minds if you have found comfort in their teachings...if you have accepted their vision...if you have accepted the inevitability of your role and punishment here on earth
For there are those among us that have served as their own laborers and have constructed their own prison...built from the inside out. They have built in imaginary comforts that they and they alone can define, comforts that keeps them confined within their walls never questioning ancient men with ancient minds that have interpreted the will of God as the reason for their confinement.

You and you alone must free yourself...as only you can walk through those doors free from walls and chains...and you and you alone must define your vision of freedom.

But for those that scream to be released from these walls and chains...I hear you...and I will stand beside you for we will now witness the strength that was placed in your body by the will of God...the strength to find your past and not let it add to your anger...the strength to confront the injustices and return to the present not seeking revenge...and the strength to continue to love me...man...any man...all men.

For I marvel at the strength that God has placed within you knowing the mountains you had climbed... the rivers you had crossed...and the dark valleys you have tread...just to stay at the side of man...any man...all men. I marvel that you do not study where life began...content in knowing that it began in you. For unlike ancient men with ancient minds...we cannot profess to know the facts of our beginning...for one can never know what came before and has very little understanding of many of the things that exist here today.

For until we release the knowledge stored in the greater portion of the brain and in the center of our heart...we will never understand the reason for our existence. It is time to abandon the selective teachings of ancient men with ancient minds and clear our thoughts, open for the invasion of the will of God...for you have value far above that calculated by man...inspite of the teachings of ancient men with ancient minds.

****

Mira did not understand why she could not go to school the same as her brother Abdul. She did not understand why she must learn to sew and to grind the meal. She did not understand why her mother permitted the elders of the village to visit and stare at her with their missing teeth, and graying hair. She had always resisted her mothers attempts to get her to stand or allow their inspection, never allowing them to pinch or squeeze her body. Her mother would always apologize and pinch her arm as she attempted to flee from the tent. When successful, she would hide and hear her mother plead with the men to return to the tent, promising that she would bring Mira back and allow them their full body inspection.

Mira did not understand where her older sister had disappeared to last year when she had reached the age of twelve, and additionally she was currently puzzled by the disappearance of her two playmates who only last week reached the same age as her sister and then they also disappeared.

On this day she had went to the river with her mother to wash clothes and on their return she had seen the donkey cart as it came up behind them on the dusty road. The driver was the same old man that had visited her mother the week before and had sat in their tent and leered at her while the mother prepared the cup of black tea. Behind the rickety cart the old man was leading two bone weary cows and one goat. The nostrils of the cows were swarming with flies and other insects and they attempted to pull the cart to the side of the road where the tall sweet grass grew.

But the donkey appeared to have his mind set against this small pleasure and so struggled to deny them the sweet morsels of grass. The rope around the animals necks were tight and, after many years, the growing neck gradually filled the rope causing depression into the skin of each of the animals. The slow steps of the lumbering cows were matched by the short choppy steps of the lone goat as it struggled against the rope that pulled it just a step behind the larger beast. As the cart pulled abreast of them, Mira's mother motioned for the man to halt as she approached the cart, firmly clutching the hand of Mira. Pulling back on the reins, the driver yanked the donkey to a standstill.

The mother covered her face with her brightly covered veil but reached down to slip Mira's veil a little lower on her face. "It's a shame to waste these fine animals on that little rag of a girl that you have selected," she said contemptuously as she reached back and pulled Mira to her side, slapping her hand as she attempted to remove a troublesome gnat from her nose. "She doesn't like me" said the old man, pointing a wrinkled grizzled finger at the young girl. "And if I take her she will just run away." The mother frowned and looked down at her frail daughter. "She will grow...she will grow, and one day she will give you much pleasure and many sons."

"You don't beat her enough and besides, the other girl will not give me trouble and will obey me and I will find much pleasure with her as she has more meat on her bones and knows how to play the flute."

The mother promised herself that she must fatten Mira as she did not want to again lose a potential husband for the girl and the loss of the badly needed cows and the goat.

Times were getting harder in the village and she needed the animals for the milk and to show that hated Rona that her daughter was more desirable than hers. It would be two years before she could trade the smallest child, who was only 8, and then she would have nothing to trade or sustain her in old age.

The old man peered at Mira through his partially closing eyes. He would love to have this child as her defiance had aroused him. " I will give you one cow and two chickens...nothing else...take it or leave it." He knew that the other woman in the small village was so anxious to trade her daughter that she would accept the remaining cow and goat as he knew of the rivalry between these two women, and in case one girl ran off he would not be left alone. He was getting much older now and would not like the thought of being deprived of the comforts of these young warm bodies, and he looked forward to having the pleasure of the two girls at one time. He would gladly trade all of his animals for this pleasure. One cow and two chickens... one cow and two chickens, thought the old woman. She lowered her eyes and muttered, knowing the answer, "At least you could throw in the goat." The old man raised his stick to start the animals, but before it could slash through the air, the woman had made up her mind. "The child is yours...take her."

****

And so the cycle continues.

NOTES

NOTES

Original art work by Warren And Yolanda Woodberry

Page 133 **"MAN AND WOMAN...WOMAN AND MAN"**

Page 135 **"MASK OF FEAR"** Rather than confront the unknown truths of religion we hide behind a mask of fear that what we have been taught is not the truth. (Relates to chapter 3)

Page 137 **"MATING GAME"** It is important that we choose a mate that is compatible. (Relates to chapter 4)

Page 139 **"ANCIENT GODS"** Ancient gods were all void of the essence of woman. (Relates to chapter 5)

Page 141 **"MATING DRUM"** God has instilled in man and woman the allure of the mating drum. (Relates to chapter 7)

Page 143 **"MOTHER AND CHILD" By Yolanda Woodberry.** Combined with a father to procreate and create life with the blessings of God. (Relates to chapter 8)

Page 145 **"THE IMAGE OF LUST"** Not to be confused or substituted for love. (Relates to chapter 9)

Page 147 **"A DIFFERENT VEIW"** Some have chosen to love their gender as a substitute for the love of the opposite sex. (Relates to chapter 13)

Page 149 **"COURTSHIP"** We are a unit...incomplete without each other. (Relates to chapter 14)

Page 151 **"SURROGATES"** There is no substitute for true love between man and woman...woman and man. (Relates to chapter 15)

Page 153 **"WATER BEARER"** Woman...the bearer of life. (Relates to chapter 16)

Page 155 **"THE CLIFF"** I have stopped here at the edge of the cliff so that we will plunge no farther. I have stopped at the edge of the cliff so that together we can see that there is no hope for us apart...divided...and un-united. (Relates to chapter 18)

MAN AND WOMAN...WOMAN AND MAN

BY: WARREN WOODBERRY

MASK OF FEAR

BY: WARREN WOODBERRY

135

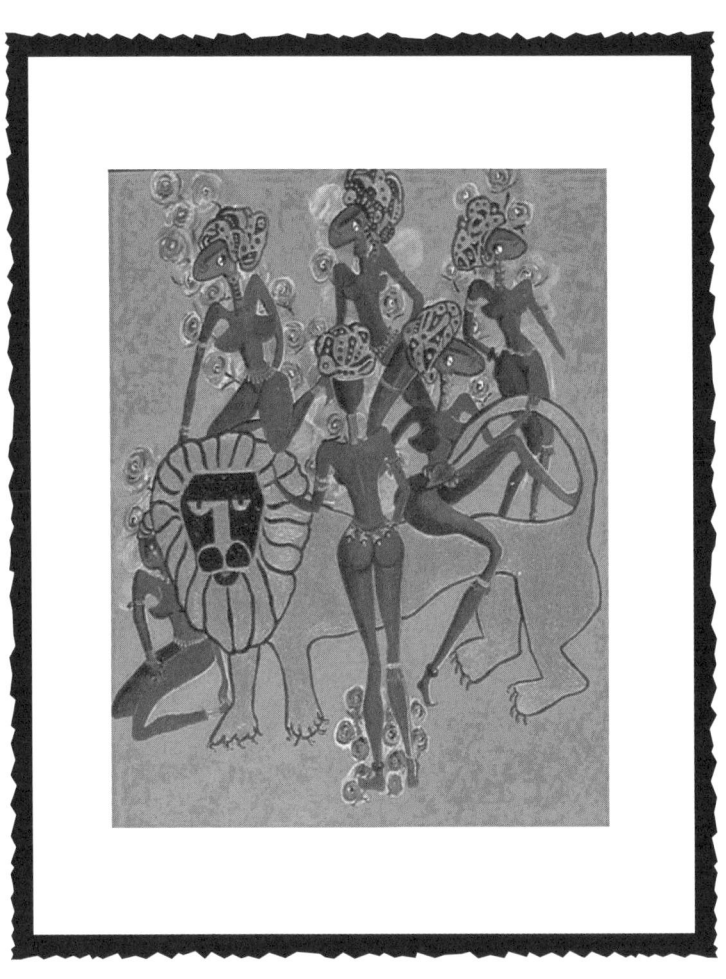

MATING GAME

BY: WARREN WOODBERRY

ANCIENT GODS

BY: WARREN WOODBERRY

MATING DRUM

BY: WARREN WOODBERRY

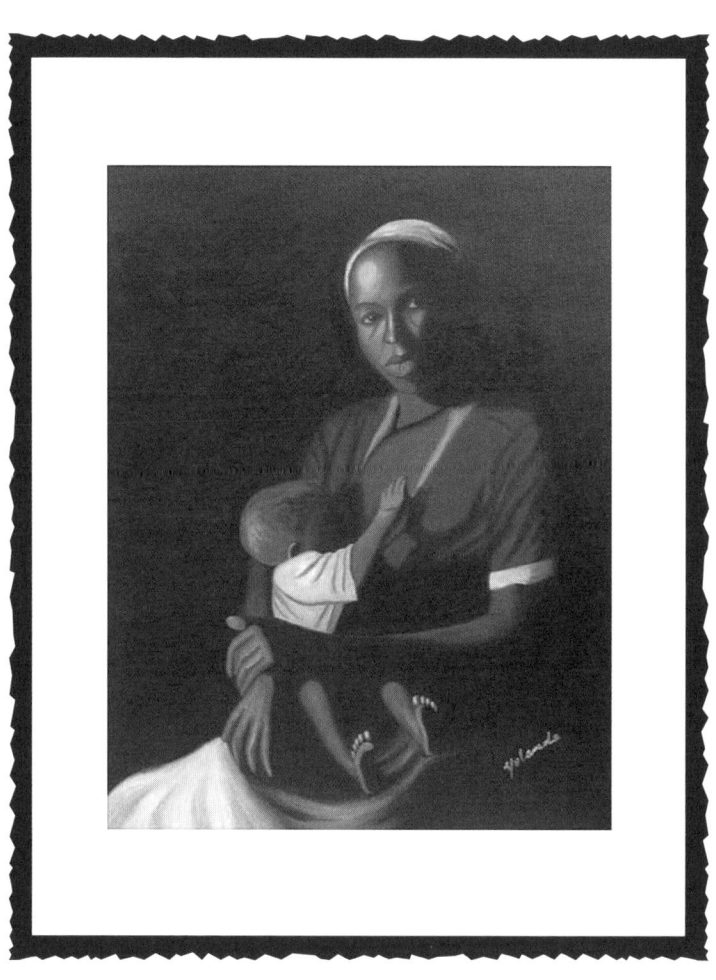

MOTHER AND CHILD

BY: YOLANDA WOODBERRY

THE IMAGE OF LUST

BY: WARREN WOODBERRY

A DIFFERENT VIEW

BY: WARREN WOODBERRY

COURTSHIP

BY: WARREN WOODBERRY

SURROGATES

BY: WARREN WOODBERRY

WATER BEARER

BY: WARREN WOODBERRY

THE CLIFF

BY: WARREN WOODBERRY

Does man desire a womb of his own? Is it that some men wish that they had never been born of woman…and so vents his anger on her body and her mind?

Is he angry with God for making her the giver of life? Do men with this thought, wish that God had been theirs, and theirs alone...all male...and needing not woman?

8
A WOMB FOR MAN

ou were taught to suppress your emotions and man was taught by ancient man with ancient minds to suppress you. But the time has come to attack this suppression and the acts of suppression.

Suppression to control must be attacked... suppression to deny the rights of others...suppression to deny a voice to others...and suppression to suppress...all must be attacked.

When man suppresses you...or children...or minorities...or intelligence...or rights...or freedom of religion...or expression...or independence...or love... he mainly suppresses himself, for some men have not realized that when you are allowed to grow it nourishes his growth and when you are granted your rights as a human...man..any man...and all men will benefit.

It is strange that man seems to enter a state of bliss and understanding when he truly experiences the will of God towards woman.

God has a great reward when man can truly achieve this understanding. Do you notice the proper fatherly attitude of a man towards his daughter and his desire to not allow her body to be defiled...to not have her raped or violated in any way? For he desires that she fall under the domination of no man.

He will not tolerate her body being viewed as merely an object of sex and degradation…he will not allow the thought of abuse and humiliation…he will not imagine gang rape...exploitation...violence... bondage...slavery and on and on. That image will be foreign to his psyche and he will want her respected for her mind and not her body, and will see beauty in her every movement…in every aspect of her womanhood, since she is the flesh of his flesh…blood of his blood… and a child of his union.

But if she is the daughter…mother…sister…or grandmother of another…then the rules morph and no longer apply…the rules of the jungle are in…and all decency and God's will are abandoned. She is humiliated...abused…and other acts, unimaginable to pay her back for the imaginary crimes of the first woman.

Does man desire a womb of his own? Is it that some men wish that they had never been born of woman and so vents his anger on her body and her mind? Is he angry with God for making her the giver of life? Do men with this thought, wish that God had been theirs, and theirs alone…all male…not needing woman at all?

Is that why some religious orders attempt to confine their priest away from God's creation of woman...but will join forces, and give absolution to members of the underworld…evil dictators...corrupt countries...the rich and the famous and pedophiles.

And in their isolation men will still seek the pleasure of woman at the expense of helpless children and those convinced that being touched by a religious leader is that same as being touched by God.

And in the homes some fathers attempt to be God like in authority, striking fear into their households as they dispense love to a minimum and authority to a maximum, in reversal of what a loving God would do. "Do as I say" they thunder while they do as they do. "Don't do as I do" they roar as they as they do things that a loving God would never do while dispensing authority where understanding is needed and fear where love is required.

Again the question must be raised...did early man desire a womb of his own?

How else can rational explain this hatred for woman that is given life by some men and some religions?

Recall the words of Augustine in 354 to 430 who would ask, "What is the difference whether it is in any woman or a mother, it is still Eve, the temptress that we must be aware of in any woman. I fail to see what use woman can be to man if one excludes the function of bearing children."

Is contact with God the preserve of man? Is interpretation of God's law reserved for man alone?

Where is it written...and by whom?

Are certain religions more fearful than others of the uniting of man and woman...woman and man? Is there this fear? Is this why there is such a resistance to woman becoming politicians...religious leaders...or even nurses or doctors? Is this the fear of man?

Is this why woman must die before allowing man to be disrespected or embarrassed? Is this why an adulteress must die...while the male equivalent can be forgiven? Is this why prostitution is a one way crime? Is this why women can still be stoned to death in some countries and banished to the wilderness in others? Is this why a woman, raped by the enemy, is to be banished or stoned to death willingly with the consent and approval of the family or the husband?

Are you confused by a story that Lot...depicted as honorable man, would offer up his daughters to a mob bent on evil. Lot is quoted as saying: "Here are my daughters: take them if you are bent on evil." 15:71

****

AND at the side of her throat and at the base of her wrist the two large veins continued to throb for there lay the site of the pulse of this woman.

And the man, drenched with the sweat of his violent attack...now satisfied from his release and violent carnal knowledge of her, was puzzled, and could no longer stand the sight of this creature...now laying helpless beneath him.

Had she...woman...any woman...all women... not been condemned in all religious scripture from the beginning of time? Had not the church accepted the fears of ancient men from ancient times that she... woman…was the cause of all the ills of the world from Pandora to Eve and beyond? Did not the religious scriptures in whatever language…from whatever country…from whatever race…since the beginning… allow and condone this disrespect…this violence?

He gazed at the throbbing pulse at her neck and then at the one on her wrist, and he knew without seeing it that the heart was synchronizing its beat…at first racing from the experience of this violent attack, causing her torn pink blouse to heave up and down in erotic and frantic spastic movements...but eventually weakening and becoming more faint by the minute.

He realized that he…man…any man...all men...had the power to stop her throbbing veins…to silence this giver of life…to silence this vessel that was similar to that of his mother who had brought him into this world. But she was not his mother…nor his sister…nor his daughter…although some of them suffered the same fate at the hands of *their* sons or husbands.

She was only woman…and a court of his peers would surely understand this act of passion…and judgement would be little if any for his attack upon this inferior being called woman. For is it not written and never censured that woman is but chattel to man?

Have not ancient men with ancient minds… called wise men…succumbed to the wishes of churches…kings and rulers and removed and edited passages from holy scriptures to their liking…but are yet to alter ancient and ungodly passages concerning the treatment of woman?

Surely this must mean that man still had the power to take her life…to take the life of the giver of life…to take the life of one who gave him life…to take the life of one whose life he could never replace.

Ancient men with ancient minds had condoned this attitude since the beginning of time. But he was confused and angry at what he had done…and he now realized that he did not know who he was when he had committed this savage criminal act.

And he was a stranger to himself…and stranger to this creature called woman that lay here beneath his feet. And his knees weakened...and he dropped to the ground beside the unconscious woman...flooded with a river of guilt and shame. Cradling her face against his, tears ran down his cheeks…mixing with the sweat from his brow, dropping finally off of his chin…forming small puddles of salty brine in the closed eyes of the woman. She stirred…and her eyes barley fluttered open as she felt his tears falling on her face. She lightly touched his head with the same hands that had only moments ago fought in vain to resist his violent attack.

He was aware that she was attempting to speak and he realized that she lacked the strength to move closer. He bent his ear to her moving lips and in a faint voice she whispered…" I forgive you…and I pray that God will forgive me for being born a woman."

****

The prayer of ancient men with ancient minds was " to be born human instead of beast...Greek instead of barbarian...and man instead of woman."

Where is it written, who wrote it and why?

For we know that God, who created all...would not allow that creation to be so lightly held.

Why is it that when men do acts of far greater magnitude it is "men will be men"? How did we get the right...how did we take the right...who said that we had the right to interpret the will of God in this manner?

Genesis Chapter 1 Verse 27: So God created man in his image (say ancient men with ancient minds) In the image of God created he him.; Male and female created he them.

Verse 28: Then God blessed <u>them</u>, and said to <u>them</u>, be fruitful, and multiply; replenish the earth and subdue it: <u>and have dominion</u> over the fish of the sea, and over the fowl of the air, and <u>over every living thing</u> that moveth upon the earth.

In reading these scriptures, it is said that God gave man and woman dominion over every living thing...but not man over woman...according to the writer.

But then...
Genesis Chapter 3 Verse 14: And the Lord said unto the serpent; upon thy belly shalt thy go, and dust shalt thou eat all the days of thy life

Verse 15: And I will put enmity (hostility, unfriendliness) between thee and the woman, and between thy seed and her seed; it shall bruise thy head, and thou shalt bruise his heel.

Verse 16: Unto the woman he said, I will greatly multiply thy sorrow and thy conception; in sorrow thou shalt bring forth children; and thy desire shall be to thy husband, <u>and he shall rule over thee.</u>

Two contradictory statements both found in Genesis.

***Genesis** Chapter 3*
Verse 17: And unto Adam he said, because you haste hearkened unto the voice of thy wife, and haste eaten of the tree, of which I commanded thee, saying thou shalt not eat of it: cursed is the ground for thy sake; in sorrow shalt thou eat of it all the days of thy life.
God then punished the snake...the woman...and the man. But man continues to punish woman as he sees fit...continuously.

Did God allow man to punish woman as he saw fit...continuously?

God punished woman with painful birth...but man's punishment of woman has gone far beyond God's wishes I am sure...for man punishes woman with a painful life before...during...and after birth.

However...in The Koran 4:, is this not the word?
O humankind! Be conscious of your Sustainer, who has created humanity out of one living entity, and out of it created its mate, and out of the two spread abroad a multitude of men and women.

"And remain conscious of God, in whose name you demand (your rights) from one another, and of these ties of kinship. Verily, God is ever watchful over you! (4.1) God is ever watchful over you!"

According to the Koran, God is ever watchful that man and woman remain conscious of God and that we are always to be aware of our ties of kinship.

Did ancient writers of ancient books differ in their love of woman. Did some hate the presence of woman in God's plan...did some wish to seek revenge for man's supposed eviction from a Garden while others gave lip service to the role of women?

This cruel display of religious interpretation must stop. It must stop for the sake of our children...our women...and for the sake of our future.

What man would accept the ancient laws of woman's place behind man while the world is being destroyed under the direction of man and man alone?

Man without woman... woman without man! It is unthinkable and unworkable...it is improbable and impossible...it is truly sacrilege that ancient men with ancient minds would attempt to separate Gods most sacred creation...man and woman and woman and man.

Sacrilege that ancient man with ancient minds would attempt to wedge a gap between the two as they attempt to insert themselves between Gods dual creation. Sacrilege as ancient men with ancient minds dictate the role of woman in today's modern world.

Attempting to place woman one step behind man...but yet sometimes becoming the first to die...in war and in peace.

Ancient men with ancient minds that could only predict the fall of mankind and the wrath of God. Ancient men that could only predict that mankind will ultimately be destroyed by an angry God. Fire and brimstone ministers that preach vengeance, hellfire and damnation. But the sermon of love and respect for you woman has yet to be universally accepted and written into most religious scriptures.

What folly to believe that ancient men with ancient minds were capable of deciphering their hallucinations and dreams while those today who profess to have the same experiences are labeled as lunatics, illusionary and madmen.

What folly to dismiss the possibility that God is capable of creating life on other planets, as mainstream scientists today still find the creation of the universe beyond their comprehension, while at the same time ancient men with ancient minds attempt to limit the power of God to create life infinitum.

And in complete contradiction, what folly to attempt the exploration and search for life on other planets...for if we cannot communicate with each other on planet earth…what communication could exist between alien beings?

God forbid that they are women.

How important are we to each other? Did God make a mistake? Was there a need for woman? Could not God have continued to create man...then animals... then animals...then man, forever?

Did God need to put woman on earth to suffer at the hands of man? Could we believe this of the God that we love? And is God satisfied just because we profess to love God and have no love to give to each other...man and woman...woman and man...as God intended?

And if there is an imbalance in woman for the need for love and the expectation of respect, is God to blame for failing to instill that ability to fulfill these needs in man...any man...all men?

9
THE FLAME OF LOVE

hat inspired this decision to be the one that would come forward attempting to declare that I...man...at last understood? That I would be the one that could accomplish what man...any man...had failed to accomplish before?

What made me decide to be the one that would ask the right questions...questions that you had wondered when a man...any man...the right man, would at last ask of you? Questions that you thought that a man...any man...the right man should always ask if he cared...if he thought...if he wanted to understand...or if he intended to love. Questions that would lead to a better understanding between any man and any woman...between the right man and the right woman.

The answer is that you were my inspiration... you woman...my woman to be. On our first meeting... your mental sate of affairs refused my attempts at penetration...so we talked...we touched...we bonded and I waited.You were very wary of penetration...but when the mechanism of your mind activated the shield of your body you allowed me to enter.

You allowed me to enter your world of discontent and find the source of this discontentment... and it was I...man...any man and all men.

Your God...my God...our God intended that we were to be one...but some men said that this is not to be. God said go together...but ancient writers...of many religions said no.

Ancient writers said let us create words of God to elevate our chosen few...and we will diminish the value of woman...any woman...all women. We will exclude woman...even though she is flesh of our flesh as we are flesh of her flesh. We will exclude woman any woman...all women...even though she is our mother...our sister...our wife or our lover. We will exclude woman even though without her we would cease to be.

And so with primitive ignorance and pagan fears...ancient men with ancient minds kept us apart.

"We are the way...the truth and the light...and no woman or man shall pass through to the Father except through us" is their slogan...but it will cost you."

And there was created a void and we were pulled apart. But then I realized that I was the void in your life...and I at last realized that you were the void in mine.

And I knew that the void in both of our lives was the love respect and understanding of each others role. And I sensed that the ancient writers were wrong and that they were not the sole interpreters of God's will...and it had not been written otherwise, as man could not write the will of God as this interpretation lies within us all.

I sensed that you had never been loved by man...any man...by the right man and that man had never been deserving of this love...this true love based on giving and receiving.

I sensed that you had never been loved enough, and that if you were to be love as expected you would return a love so strong that it would compel one to love you in return...just as strong.

The desire to love was still strong in you...still warm...still hopeful...still open ...still possible. This desire lies in all women because it was God's edict that you were to be loved and protected.

If God were not capable of keeping this promise to you...what chance did mortal man have of keeping this vow?

Is it feasible that ancient man with ancient minds would not be capable of describing the intensity of your pain...the height of your passion nor the feeling of motherhood, but yet he would attempt to define your God and the treatment reserved for you?

In addition...if man could disobey God and disregard the concept of a loving God, then why could you not do the same...and compress your life giving chamber and refuse to multiply and provide the source of the continuation of life?

You had escaped from a loveless relationship before the fires turned your ability to love into ashes...before there was no fire to rekindle...before the ashes turned cold. And there was a slight flame that glowed in your body...guiding me...man...the right man...to your dimming light. I sensed that there was hope that the fire would burn again...and I...man...not any man...but the right man...would never leave you surrounded by darkness once that flame was rekindled.

Your low flame of a love...still searching for a blaze caught me and made me aware that I had the striker...and that my brush with you would bring forth the flame that you seek...that I had the wind that could cause the blaze of our love to become the ultimate fire...God's intended fire...between man and woman...woman and man.

How important are we to each other, or did God make a mistake? Was there a need for woman or could God not have continued to create man...then animals, then man forever? Did God need to put woman on earth to suffer at the hands of man? Could we believe this of the God that we love? And is God satisfied just because we profess to love God...and have no love to give to each other...man and woman...woman and man...both creations of this same God.

If there is an imbalance in woman for the need for love and the expectation of respect...is God to blame for this high expectation that man would love...honor and that both would obey the directives placed in their heart by God?

Did God fail to link these needs and expectations of woman with the needs and expectations of man...and did God fail to program man to these needs? If this can be proven, that God was deficient then I will accept man's pleas of ignorance.

I will accept man's ignorance of the difference between right and wrong in ancient times...when the mind was primitive and easily deceived.

I will forgive man for revisions...alterations abridgements...additions...embellishments...inclusions and exclusions when in this pagan state of ignorance, for the bases of man's religion were built on the very roots of paganism which were nourished and fed by ancient men with ancient minds.

But today we cannot accept man's inability to correct the misinformation of ancient man's interpretations of ancient scripture...we cannot continue to allow for the continued injustices to you...woman...any woman...all women...for that is asking far beyond our comprehension to understand why.

For man still holds the key and he must decide how important to the survival of this world is woman, for his value is intrinsically tied to hers and her development.

For now is truly the time to revise...to alter...to abridge...to add...to embellish...to include...and exclude.

And now is truly the time to acknowledge that man professed what he could not know...that man decreed what he did not understand...that man controlled what he had no right to control.

For man said where God was...while not knowing...man confirmed why God was...while not knowing...and man attempted to control all acts of God while having no right to separately control or decipher.

For ancient men with ancient minds have no right to control the love of man for woman or the love of woman for man. They have no right to direct the love of man from woman and no right to direct the love of woman from man, and absolutely no right to control our love of God.

For some men have seen the light...some men have *again* deciphered the will of God...and some men have *again* decided that it is time to acknowledge man's intellect and not be guided by his superstitious fears.

Ancient men with ancient minds declared that they now knew that Heaven was not an inverted bowl over the earth...as thought by Homer...and that Hades was not on the undersides of earth and unlit by the sun.

In Hesiod it was believed that night was a substance that welled up from under the earth...while Orpheus declared that a primeval egg was birthed by the Gods and that the upper half became heaven.

Early man mystified by the sun, the moon and the stars, decided that he knew where the Gods lived... he knew where the Gods played...and he knew how the Gods interacted with man.

Early Greeks credited the sky gods with the running of the earth according to their whims and fancies and that they played with early man as toys, while riding fiery chariots back and forth like subway trains, lusting after and capturing the daughters of man...impregnating them and convincing them that the act was performed by a swan or some other mystical figure. And man, then as now, cannot separate fact from fiction...reality from dreams.

They saw Gods descend to earth from the heavens...and believed that the sun was closer to the earth than the moon.

Aristotle and others conceived of the world as being flat and that it floated on a bed of air like a leaf...but were confronted with a contradiction by Thalus of Miletus in 585 BCE, who contended that the world was not flat but floated on a bed of water.

At that time it was taught that man was at his peak of intelligence and thought to be more than qualified to define the workings of God and the creation of man and woman, but yet today he can not comprehend how the pyramids were built.

And ancient men with ancient minds knew even less about love. Love was stifled in our beginning by ancient men with ancient minds but still lay dormant within us today, refusing to die. This dormant love has weathered the onslaught of ancient men who have acted as paid assassins. What perverts love…what destroys love…and why does love die...or never even live? What is the science of love…since there is science to every living thing?

What do the great thinkers say about love in the many books of love and what do the men of science say? Those men that profess to be able to explain all things...some like ancient men with ancient minds that probably never loved...men that have never been loved…these men that deny love…these men that know love only as a stranger.

These ancient men sat in isolation...in isolated places, void of the touch of woman...void of the love of woman...void of the meaning of woman... void of woman yesterday..today...and tomorrow...all designing methods to punish woman for the expulsion from an imaginary garden.

Ancient men who would recoil from the touch of woman...but yet encourage and allow the heavy hand of man to strike her down and rob her of her dignity. Men that have never known the love of a woman or of any human being.

Men who were only touched by the cold hand of power and the desire to remove the life-giving hand of God from the affairs of the world and replace it with their life taking hand.

Ministers of religion that profess to know God's will…that profess that the way to God is through them…that God speaks to them and them alone…men that attempt to take God's children as their own… seeking the praise that God deserves?

Ancient man builds his heavens here on the earth that God promised to you and I…man and woman…woman and man. We must understand that ancient men with ancient minds has neither permission from you or I...man or woman...woman or man...or from God.

Genesis 1:28 *"And God said unto them, be fruitful, and multiply, and replenish the earth, and subdue it."*

And man agreed…but added, "Give me your sons, who I will send to their death by the thousands for my causes…both large and small…fickle or vain…for riches and for power as I see fit."

Thousands will die to build a wall…to build a temple…to build a bridge…to protect my border…to erect my tomb…to avenge my honor…because they are the wrong color, race or religion and because they have been deemed to be dispensable.

God said subdue the world…and man attempts to destroy it.

Life is not sacred.

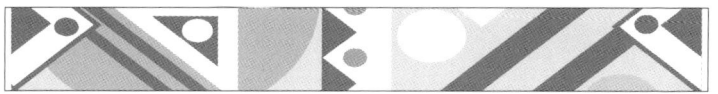

10
LIFE IS NOT SACRED TO MAN

en forced many of you to abandon hopes for the returned love of man...for some heard you not, as they attempted to ignore your needs of love which is the only source of life's continuation here on earth.

A love, which was promised by God...but ignored by man. This mating of the sexes promised by God, but aborted by man.

You, woman, knelt on the bare ground and prayed to God for the strength to survive...the strength to understand...and the strength to fulfill your role.

While you prayed on bare ground and while you prayed to God for deliverance from the degradation of man...man built churches and temples on that ground...churches and temples that he thought would reach the sky...churches and temples that sought to pierce the heavens...new towers of Babel. Churches and temples that were on God's land...but for the glory of man and man alone.

Churches and temples built for women to glorify man...churches and temples built for man to glorify man...churches and temples built to let you in...and to lock God out. For God needed not the walls of the church...but man did.

Churches that interfere with the direct communications to God. "Speak to God through me... they imply" man says… "Complain of me through me" they say..."Interpret God's design for woman through me", man. "Speak not directly to God for I am now the way…if it were not so, I would have told you. I am the way…the truth and the light…for no man cometh to the father except through me."

Man became a self elected prophet…some became the son of God...while others were self elected as messengers of God. Divided in their concept of God...they were untied in the treatment of woman. "Woman must not preach…say some…must not teach…must not be ordained…must not lead...and must not interpret God's will…and woman must not rise above man or equal to "…says man.

While man sets your limitation he also sets his own…and when he sets his own…he sets the limitations of the world at the same time.

Genesis 1:28 "And God said unto them, be fruitful, and multiply, and replenish the earth, and subdue it."

And man agreed…but added, "Give me your sons, who I will send to their death by the thousands for my causes…both large and small.."

And thousands will die to build a wall to build a temple…to build a bridge…to protect a border…to erect a tomb…to avenge someone's honor…because they are the wrong color, race or religion or because they have been deemed to be dispensable."

183

God said, subdue the world...and man attempts to destroy it.

Life is not sacred to man.

You gave life...and man took life...in war...in greed and in ignorance. Man took the lives of the unborn...the new born...and the born again.

He took the lives of the young...the middle aged...and the elderly without discrimination, all in the name of religion. And untold thousands more will die for failure to honor and worship man's chosen God... who you and I...man and woman...can freely choose...and call by any name...since there is but one true God.

Life is not sacred to man.

Religions that use the force of armies to instill their religion...religions that imposed their God on others through fear of death...and they still use these forces today in the name of their chosen God. A God that common sense dictates could not possibly approve of their methods.

For if God...your God...my God...our God...a benevolent God...had wanted this form of acknowledgement from us...there would be no need for a battlefield of dying young men...with bodies separated from families...with bodies separated from homes...with bodies separated from limbs and with bodies separated from life. For if this state was pleasing to God then it would have been easier to have humans born torn...mangled and dead.

Man put man…woman…and child to death for not worshiping the God that he chose...and man chose hundreds of God's throughout the world...and then put woman to death for not worshiping man…any man and all men.

The God of the land today is declared the anti-Christ of tomorrow by the conquering army...and the God declared the anti-Christ today will be restored by an avenging army tomorrow...as God is used to justify man's inhumanity to man...and is dragged across borders at the whim and fancy of conquering armies.

There is no "How to Book" to reach a God consciousness…for why would the God that can program us all need to write a book?

And if there were need for written scriptures... who would allow them to stand unadulterated and what race...culture or religion would resist the urge to re-write them according to their customs or their goals?

Would the Essenes in BC not have their version…and what would be found in the Apocrypha hidden works that the church decided should remain hidden from the world?

Would not the Jews, the Christians, the Church of Rome, writers translating from Aramaic to Hebrew to Greek to Latin then to English, alter most of their original concepts, as words, customs, interpretations, likes, dislikes, prejudices, angers, hatreds and racisms would contribute to alter their meanings?

Would the Hindu text be merely the hand of man in writing the four Vedas and the "Song of God," which is a message of the Upanishads and the Hindu philosophy which contains instructions to God Krishna.

And there are the tablets given to Moses for the Christians and the Jews...and the Koran which is a transcript of a tablet preserved in Heaven and revealed to the Prophet Muhammad by the Angel Gabriel. And one must not forget the inspiration that came to Buddha as he meditated under a banyan tree where he was illuminated and the truth came to him.

As they mix and match...and match and miss, all will say that *their* scripture is the word of God...and let no dog bark.

So many words...so many meanings...so much anger...so much vengeance and so little love.

Are the followers of the Hindu religion closer to a truth as they profess to believe that there is but one God and that God is incomprehensible and beyond the understanding of humans? That God has no known recognizable form, space or time. Would this concept, if adopted, ease the conflict of attempts to portray God in our own image, disallowing a concept and a conflict about whether God was black, white or yellow... Muslim, Christian or Buddhist...blue-eyed or brown.

Is there no limit to the wars and religious conflicts that will continue to alter our path to God consciousness? Is there no limit to the riches accumulated to be poured into the pockets of architects for new gleaming towers of Babel while we cannot feed our brothers or sisters here on earth?

They then concoct stories of the evilness of woman...the evilness of Pandora...the wickedness of Clytemnaestra...Medea...Phaedra...Electra... Aphrodite...Helen of Troy. And many hundreds or thousands of years later, Eve became the cause of the shame of man...passing the blame for the evils of the world to you woman...any woman...all women.

Is it not obvious that the concept that women are second class and men have a right to lord over them was earlier found in the teachings of the Greek philosophers Socrates and Plato...many many years BC...and later adopted by ancient men with ancient minds, who have done tremendous damage with this adopted consensus?

Who will come forward and destroy the myth of the fall of man? Who will come forward and resist this continued myth...handed down by the historians of old and allowed to disenfranchise one half of God's creation?

It will be you and I...man and woman...woman and man as we clear our minds of ancient men with ancient minds in order to absorb the true will of God. As we clear our minds of ancient stories that stretch the imagination, asking us to accept the unacceptable and to believe the unbelievable.

It must be you and I...man and woman... woman and man...for it is not to late. For it is obvious that we can not know the reason nor the time of our beginning.

For if God is to enter our minds and our souls they must not be filled with unresolved conflicts. Conflicts created by man's interpretations of religion... conflicts resulting in confusing stories as all history is contaminated with the fiction of ancient man...conflicts to determine who came first my tribe or yours...my father or yours...my nation or yours...your God or my God.

Our children's minds must be clear to hear and feel the spirit of God unburdened with ancient mindset and religious dogma.

Dogma learned by repeating and repeating...by reading and re-reading...by accepting and not questioning...by hearing but not feeling...by filling our minds with the history of man and his record of religious wars as we are bombarded from the cradle to the grave...leaving no room to allow the loving personal instructions of God. Dogma which merely qualifies us to claim membership in a social order, otherwise known as religion.

Many have been guilty of accepting accounts of God that the presenter has long since abandoned, revised or altered. Floods and insects became became the tools of prophets...natural disasters became signs of Gods displeasure...as all nature was interpreted by some race somewhere as an act of their Gods annoyance with humanity.

Religious scriptures have lost their ability to unite and are sources of divisiveness and conflict throughout the world.

Let us *open* our eyes and look and feel the direction of God...direct from the source and not a revised edition...a source void of man's account of vengeance by your God...my God...and our God.

We must open our minds with a new beginning...receptive to new love...and a new understanding of our role here on earth.

We must clear our minds of *his*tory and allow room for *our*story...man and woman...woman and man...for all we need to know of God will come directly from the source.

Must we remember the words of a native in South Africa who said, "When the missionaries first came to Africa they had the Bible and we had the land. They then said, 'Let us pray' and we closed our eyes. When we opened them again, we had the Bible...and they had the land."

But some religions and their doctrines will not only take the land...they will take one's soul and lead one far from true communication with the creator while making claims in the name of God. Some religions will not only claim their right by might, but will suggest that they have heavenly authority.

Some religions claim to possess land by a God given right...but yet have need of barbed wire, ultra modern weapons of destruction, and armed guards to defend them from weaponless women and children throughout the world. And they destroy the very works of creation created by God...sending them back to God as lifeless victims in the name of religion.

Would your God...my God...or our God condemn us to follow the conflicting teachings of ancient men with ancient minds and not allow us direct communications to the spirit and commands set forth for a better life...free from the conflicts of man's petty attempts to be God.

While some use religion to define who we are within a culture, a race or a nation...we defy God who has already defined our status. Some still leave the presence and protection of God to seek the presence and protection of men in fancy robes or silk suits.

The worship of God has now been reduced to theatre by ancient men with ancient minds...and the stage is set...religion is now a production made for television.

It is time to uplift God's creation and leave the mysteries of creation to ancient men with ancient minds. It is time to be thankful for life and the ability to live...thankful for man and thankful for woman... thankful for creation, from whatever the source, and thankful that you can reproduce life... share life...and have a life to live.

I ask you to look closely at your sisters...your mothers and your grandmothers and if you see happiness in their eyes and you feel contentment in their souls...then ask them the way to this bliss with man...any man...all men.

But if you see sadness in their eyes and sense unhappiness in their souls...your personal journey must begin.

For they will not have known the feeling of love between man and woman...woman and man.

For they will have sacrificed their life for faith...and for a reward that will never came...for they were the fodder for ancient men with ancient minds.

11
THE TEMPLE OF GOD

s it God's will that man must now be made to realize the value of this gift to the world? Is it God's will that man now realizes his mistakes and seeks the solution to the world's problems wherever they may be found? Is it now God's will that man and woman rekindle and rethink the intended relation between you and I...man and woman...woman and man?

Has man realized that the concept of religion has never worked? Has man realized that the rules of early religious orders were founded for the purpose of controlling...suppressing and manipulating the multitudes in order to bring them under the control of ancient men with ancient minds? And that their teachings, then as now, had very little to do with God and more to do with making them appear to be God-like and to request the same reverence due to God.

Will man ever realize that his methods, universally used, will not solve our problems? Will man realize that religious persecution...the gun...the bombs...the intolerance...the wars...the violence... slaughter...the enslavement...and terrorism is not the way?

Can not the present military and religious leaders learn from past histories, and see that they will only leave the same legacy of conflicts if they continue to support these ancient men with ancient ideas? Can they not see that the suppression of women is suppression for us all?

Was man's interpretation of ancient laws relegating women to second-class, the first instance where we went wrong?

Man…in his futile efforts to equate with God… to be God like…to be God_has attempted to change woman's role here on earth.

Man has attempted to make woman a square peg in a round hole…making sure she does not fit into his scheme to be God-like…or his scheme to be God. He has excluded one half of the intelligence provided by God…one half of the love needed…one half of the compassion needed…and one half of what God gave to the planet earth. And more importantly...one half of the source needed for continued life.

Can any religion that uses the sword for vengeance and retribution be a true religion? Can we forgive or accept religions that gained their prominence by the sword and still today maintain it's power by economic and political strangulation? Would not religions that experienced this type of oppression in days gone by call for God to come to their aid and part their sea of oppression?

In your search would you understand the role of the Emperor Constantine in 324 CE? Would there be any truth to the role he played in spreading his chosen and newly adopted religion by force? Would he have combined the might of the Roman army with his desire to control the worship of man and woman...and woman and man in an attempt to be the first ruler who combined church and state

Who then orchestrates the ceremony of religion...God...or man? Who is religion for...God or man? Who are the temples for...God or man? For since God has designated our bodies as temples that only we can defile...can there be need for another?

We were, at first, spectators of religious conflicts that were confined to members of the church. Conflicts expanded to now include innocent victims whose only crime was that they were in the wrong place at the wrong time. And we are all now subjected to religious wars and conflict that take the life of the innocent.

Conflicts, as pagan rites battled with pagan rites...as astronomers clashed with soothsayers...as witchcraft opposed men of science and as the chemistry of religion was formed. Conflicts, as the Orthodox Jews fought to retake the city of Jerusalem from the Romans...disharmony between the Jewish Orthodox religion and the early Christians, as the Jews sought to disassociate themselves from the concept of Jesus.

Conflicts, as Muslims, Hindus, Christians and Buddhists, all shared external and internal conflicts among their own faith as even brothers in religion could not agree on the concept of God and differed in their interpretation of their chosen religious expressions...but yet, all calling for the assistance of the one that could give them invincibility. All calling for the aid of the "One True God" and all attempting to persuade the multitudes that this "One True God" was on their side.

Ancient men who declared that to write the name of God was a sin...(as they took the lives of your sons and daughters, which was no sin) and those that questioned their word, were to be punished by death as ancient men attempted to act as the chosen executioner for God...your God...my...our God.

Conflicts, as each religion fought to establish the historical period when it's Gods, ancestors, saviors and heroes established the bases of their religion. Conflicts as each religion or nation declared that they were the beginning of civilization. During this period varied and conflicting religious opinions were written and taken as gospel by their believers and followers.

Buddhism began with the enlightenment of the Buddha, as did Islam with the revelation of the Koran to the prophet Muhammad, while Judaism was defined by the great exodus from Egypt and the deliverance of the law at Mt. Sinai. Christianity built its premises on the incarnation of God in Jesus Christ whose teachings and resurrection from the dead served the same purpose.

Conflicts, as the Church of Rome dictated the writings of the disciples as fact, when there was more fiction than fact...more memory than accuracy...more myth than truth...more legend than history...more plagiarism from pagan religions than from a true communication with the spirit of God. Conflicts in the translations of Greek and Hebrew versions

Back and forth...forth and back...but mostly backwards.

Would the Greek philosophers, such as Plato, deny that their culture and the advocacy of love between men of intellect, engraved homosexuality in stone, seeking to deny any value or intellect to woman?

Would the Greek philosophers be the first to declare that woman brought sin and trouble to the world in the form of Pandora...claimed by them to be the first woman on earth, who opened her box and loosed evils on the world, long before Eve even knew that a tree had apples and that serpents were not to be trusted?

And would many religions, hundreds and thousands of years later adopt many of these same concepts about women and incorporate them into Judaism, Islam and Christianity.

With the confusion of interpretation, would it even be possible to find a bag of gold, buried 10 feet away, following a map with such a tortuous path of revisions, superstitions, myths, ignorance, deviousness and wickedness as the interpreters of some religious scriptures have created?

And ancient minds with ancient thoughts declare that they and they alone are the recorders of the word of God! Are not all religions guilty of using the historical concept of God as a personal tool of war... declaring that God gave them the right to wage war on non-believers?

And is there not a basic acknowledgement inherent in all men and women that there is a source responsible for the creation of all things in our life...but religions battle for the copyright? Will not the shepherds of these multi-faiths continue to herd their flock to the slaughter in the name of their one true God? The word of God will not be heard by those who wage religious wars...as the sound of God will be but a whisper...lost to the sound of the gun...so we must leave these armies of ancient men with ancient minds as they write their manuals of war in the guise of religious scriptures...all supposedly in the name of their one true God.

We must...you and I...man and woman...woman and man...begin to realize that we must discontinue being used as fodder for these conflicts over the interpretation of the will of God.

For man is incapable of knowing the will of the creator, as his pen would be poised to re-interpret any passage that spoke of love or respect.

Religions that swear that God has given them the word. This word, if given, that could never survive the years of alteration for the glorification of man.

I would now ask you...were any of *these* the hand of God...your God...my God...our God?

Some revisions were ordered by kings, queens, military rulers, the church, conquering armies or by scribes...scholars...printers...and publishers. In England, revisions of the Bible_by law_rested in the hands of the Crown during the reign of Queen Elizabeth I.

Were any of *these* revisions the hand of God?

And in all of these revisions. for thousands of years...these revisers could not_would not_did not, revise the concept of the treatment of you...woman... any woman...all women.

And your blame and shame was in the very ink that supposedly transferred the word of God from pen to paper...traveling throughout the ages...unchanging and unending.

But man could only re-write what he was instructed to write by ancient men with ancient minds... all void of God's vision of you, woman. And although myths could be added, legends included and fables inserted, woman would remain woman.

St. Chrysostom declared woman as "a necessary evil...a natural temptation...a desirable calamity...a domestic peril...a deadly fascination and a painted ill!"

And while womanism was defined as the cause of evil...man continued his search for more "ism's" to define his *Confusionism*.

Adwaitism...Albigensianism...Alcoranism... Amidism...Anabaptism...Anglicanism... Anglo-Catholicism...Aniconism...Arianism... Augustianism...Baalism...Beism...Brahmanism... Buddhism...Calvinism...Catholicism...Christianism... Confucianism...Consubtantialism...Creationism...and this only covers from A to C

The path to understanding the will of the creator cannot be found in this man-made maze of -isms or on these battlefields of religious wars...for the price is too dear.

There are those who have the strength and the awareness of God within their souls to stop at the gates of this madness...and realize that enough is enough and it must be you and I...man and woman...woman and man. For we must withdraw and repair to our original cave to reunite, while the battle for the throne of God rages among these tribal religions. And by the grace of the creator we will emerge unscathed from our place of isolation and love...ready to complete the will of God to live in peace and harmony...you and I...man woman...woman and man.

We will not give 10% for the building of religious temples that glorify man and defy God. We will not give one day per week to the false praising of a man-made creator and give six days to hate, religious wars and the annihilate of Gods creation.

We will seek council from both man and woman whenever their intellect and goodness is recognized, as you will teach me…to teach you…to teach me…in a never-ending cycle of learning.

I ask you to look closely at your sisters..your mothers and your grandmothers...and if you see happiness in their eyes...and you feel contentment in their souls...then ask them the way to this bliss with man...any man...all men. But if you see sadness in their eyes...and sense unhappiness in their souls...your journey must begin.

For they will not have known the feeling of love between man and woman...woman and man.

For they will have sacrificed their life for faith and for a reward that never came...for they were the fodder for ancient men with ancient minds.

God's word cannot be found in mass meetings or at gatherings at man made holy places…for these gatherings will not allow us to think…to pray…and to have peace of mind...for what is holy land to one man…is a funeral ground for another.

For my mind tells me that God would not allow any religion that utilized the sword to establish itself to set the path to the one true God!

If it is God that we seek…we must come together…you and I…man and woman…woman and man for together we are the only ones to define this road.

12
SHARED BLAME

ut enough of this…for we do not truly know the will of God…and man's interpretation has gotten us into failure after failure…conflict after conflict and war after war…and death after death.

But take no satisfaction in this seemingly blanket condemnation of man…for you too must share the blame…share the guilt…share the cost.

Some are guilty by having stepped back and permitted this to happen.

You have, in some cases submitted, and while man went about his daily task of destroying men… women…children…and the world, you,passive woman of this world, studied and accepted ancient ways in a modern world.

You have become content…content to serve man as a second-class citizen, and you then watched as man made laws destroyed the rights of others…not knowing that man was creating the base that would also, one day, deny you. But you did not care as long as you believed your position was secured.

Man then placed some of you on a pedestal... while others were buried underneath.

And men lost their lives...because of you, but yet you wonder who is to blame?

Did you accept this placement...did you question this placement...did you attempt to elevate other women to this elevated position...or did you just blindly accept your elevation while knowing that you should not be there alone and that injustices were done to others to protect your good image?

Did the blood of the mother of Salome race through your veins and did you desire vengeance...did you require revenge...did you require the power to cause the death of others?

In your desire to appease man and to make a secure place for yourself, some of you accepted a lesser role in life. Regardless of the corruption on the throne... regardless of the injustices in the court...regardless of the brutality in the country...regardless of the innocence of the accused...you accepted these injustices to be safe...to be secure...to share the throne.

Caring not how your silence contributed to these injustices.

You felt secure that locks, fences, bars, and chains, surrounding your manicured lawns, would keep the hate out and the love in, but you soon found that locks,fences, bars and chains worked both ways...as they prevented entry and exit.

Some of you were locked in as possessions...
some of you were fenced in to establish your
boundaries...and some were chained to a loveless life...
for life.

We must stave off this cancer...ever feeding at
our emotions...ever feeding at our ability to love...
insatiably feeding at our tables throughout the world...
leaving us starving for the love of our brothers and our
sisters. And as individuals over came the differences in
race, color, economic status and education, ancient man
with ancient minds condemns this relationship with a
vengeance.

Shall we overcome? We shall over come.
Can we overcome? We can over come.

And you and I...man and woman...woman and
man...are the spoils of war as we attempt to dance to
their every tune. And while we shuffle to their tune...
they would have us dance far from the music of your
God...my God...our God.

God created you…woman...as a companion of
man…hoping that together…this world would be a
better place. But man has, with your consent and
non-protesting behavior, placed you, God's work,
aside...and we will never know what the world would
have become had you been an equal partner in the
affairs of the world from time beginning.

But for now...today...woman must equally set
policy…and that policy must be for the salvation of the
world…for your sons and daughters…for their sons and
daughters…and for their sons and daughters.

You…woman must not enter the arena now…at this time…as another complication to the world's problems…but as a solution, for the problems of the world must be contained…for they are too many and too frequent.

You, woman, must enter the arena to repair... to balance…to assist…to mold…to inform…to teach... to create…to love and to give hope. You woman… must help re-unite the world and once again fall in love with man…any man…the right man. By awareness... involvement…and love, all things can be as God planned.

The man made laws of our planet must give way to more compassionate laws…laws for the good of all...laws not just for the mighty…laws not just for the ego of man…laws not just for the sake of control, and not laws to continue to suppress the spirit, soul and rights of others in the name of religion.

In the past man used his power to fight the elements and the wild beast of the forest…he used his energy to fight the land…to feed his family…he used his energy to fight the elements of the sea…and he used his energies to halt the encroachment of the enemy. Brute strength and force were the leadership qualities of ancient times, however, today there is an enemy of a different sort…based on pure power, greed, and with a new violence and a new deception...and man needs to combine his strength and force with the strength and force of woman to combat the enemy of today.

It is time that you sit in council with man and determine another course…another view…another choice. Now is the time to halt this world of misunderstanding…mistrust...misgivings and misfortune.

Now is the time to enter the fray…now is the time to start anew…now is the time to make amends for your absence.. Now is not too late…too early or too hopeless. Now is the time…now is the opportunity and now is where and when we must begin.

But your change will not come overnight…as there will be those that will still resist your coming… they will resist your guidance…they will resist your inclusion...and they will be both man and woman… woman and man.

Men will deny you …and women will defy you. They will take your desires for peace and harmony and turn it into weapons to be turned back into your bosom.

You must start with your children…speak to them of love and of temperament…of understanding and of fairness…of brother and of sister…of man and of woman. And speak to them of God.

For we are all to blame...you and I…man and woman…woman and man...for we have not learned how to decipher God for ourselves.

God did not create man to join warring religious groups...with the sole purpose of destroying Gods creation in Gods name!

Ancient men grab the innocent and those easily led...they then use them as fodder now that they have realized the power of control. Believers that do not possess independent thought...sheep like...a flock...led by whomever takes the lead...whether a good shepherd or bad. Blind believers led by blind faith...unquestioned loyalty as they sing, "Give me that old time religion, its good enough for me."

But its not good enough for some...as we have now seen the manipulative value it serves for ancient interpreters of religion. Religion created by man to elevate man...for God did not create religion!

The Creator had a simple plan for you and I...man and woman...woman and man...but scribes and holy men could not abide such simple reasoning...for where would they be in this scenario. You and I...man and woman...must withdraw from this farce and find peace in God's true meaning.

Can the first step to find love and understanding begin on the battlefield or on the pulpit of religious differences? I think not...for love will not find a place on these man made altars.

This mass pursuit for multiple religious interpretations will not abate soon, if ever, but there is hope that a movement can begin to see the folly of this exercise...and that movement is the love between you and I...man and woman...woman and man.

And it is hoped that a small but significant move will be made...to realize the value of resolving the differences between the sexes...in this imperfect world...which gets more imperfect day by day.

The responsibility to begin to love is with us both…man and woman…woman and man...in our own definition of duality.

Ancient man has had centuries of interpreting ancient text...centuries of defining our role...our love...our hate...our need...our goal...our destiny. The interpreters of paganism and magic have now attempted to take on the role of God...your God...my God...our God.

Will we continue to allow them to experiment and manipulate with our beliefs? Will we continue to allow them to forge myths into legends...legends into reality...reality into legends and legends back into myths?

Over time they will make the improbable probable...the supernatural natural...fusing them all...not allowing us to know the difference between right and wrong...or wrong or right. Declaring us to be wrong when we are truly right...and declaring themselves to be right when they are truly wrong, not allowing some to know the difference between one or the other.

I speak to you now and present a start for your journey. I spare no means to present these questions to those among you who wish to define their past. I implore those of you with an inquiring mind to decide for yourself...and to confront ancient man with ancient

For I too am confused as myth became legend...and legend became reality...as the history of one nation...became the history of humanity. As world history was replaced with the history of one nation...and the will of God was replaced with the words of man.

For ancient men with ancient minds can no longer be trusted to define our history...for he has failed to define his own. He argues over borders and ancient sites...over what God said and to whom...where God said it and why...how God said it and when...and if God said it and what it means.

Reckless of truth...generous with errors...man spreads his craft with unplausable beliefs.

Ancient men with ancient minds do not teach love...nor do they preach love. It is time that we...you and I...man and woman...woman and man, take our future in our hands, for our eyes must see through these shadows of deceit, confusion...violence...disrespect... mysticism and misinterpretations.

We can no longer allow for this misinformation to continue. We can no longer allow the continued misinterpretation of the value of love and respect between women and men...and men and women. If love is a mystery, then we will solve it together as man and woman...woman and man and only God will decide the outcome.

Leviticus 12: 2 - *"If a woman hath conceived seed , and born a man child : then she shall be unclean for 7 days;"*

And in *Leviticus 12: 5*- *"But if she bear a maid child, then she shall be unclean for two weeks."*

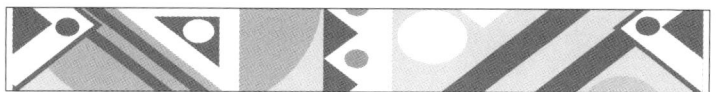

13
SUBSTITUTE FOR MAN

oman...for I know you are woman...I know you...but in some way...I feel that I do not.

Why are you so alien to me...man...any man...all men? Why do you appear so alien to me when I should know you?

I see that you do not want me to touch you... but that is because the shield of ignorance has fallen over your eyes...for you now see me as the enemy of woman...for you now attempt to take my place...with woman...any woman...with all women.

But I am a messenger from man...his conscious so to speak...an emissary...making the first step that must be made by one of us...if this madness is to ever end.

I see you are still woman...even though you adopt a somewhat different posture. Are you me...are you man...are you woman? You have taken a choice to love woman as man...to be man for woman...confusing both woman...man...and God.

You have taken a choice to take the place of man...and love yourself. Who is to blame for your adaptation...man...any man...all men?

The blame lies with man's inability to love you as he should…he is to blame for not nourishing the love between man and woman...between woman and man. His touch was not the touch you needed…his touch was not the touch of love...for his touch was the touch of hate…of violence and of possession. Your touch was the reminder to man of man's imagined rejection from God.

And so you have adopted this man-challenging role. But I will not judge…for I come not as a judge... for you felt a need…and you filled that need that you saw for some...but still left a gap for others And other women…any woman…and all women can still respond to the touch of man…any man…all men. And any man can respond to the touch of woman...any woman...all women.

I have come to show you that we have a common platform from which to start anew...for we both love woman…any woman…all women.

And you are still woman, even though you adopt a different stance and a different posture. You love woman as I do...both physically and mentally.

Come…for it is important that I hear your story…for if you and I...man and woman...woman and man...are to meld into one...you must tell me of your source of rebellion...for your point of view will be of the utmost importance to my journey to re-unite man and woman…any man...any woman...all men and all women.

For we must unite with love and respect for each other if we are to unite the world as God intended. Show me what man…any man…all men must do to rectify this need you feel to vilify him and his treatment of you…woman.

Show me the way to diffuse your anger and rebuild your need. Show me the way to touch…to feel and to respect and connect…to love and to earn your love in return. To reverse the direction in which we spin on a collision course…destined to destroy all life…if we do not learn to love again.

Can you place aside your anger for a moment… can you reach out and touch me…and speak to me…of this hurt that you feel? Will our touch uncover the need that we both have for each other?

You say that man…any man…all men have brutalized you…woman…and that you have taken your self into your own arms to repair the pain…and you have loved yourself.

But you have been correct in your deciphering of man and his treatment of you…woman…any woman all women.

Man has indeed brutalized woman...any woman...all women. Man has brutalized man...any man...all men and man has brutalized children… animals and is guilty of self-abuse.

You have now vowed that no man will ever again enter your body…or penetrate…or violate…or subjugate.

Fear not…for that is not my goal. My goal is to halt this downhill race of self destruction between the sexes…because in this race there can be no checkered flag for either of us. For our coffin marking the place where true love has died...will only share a black flag of death.

So let us just be here…as one…in complete darkness...for we are not yet ready for the light…for light will show the extent of our shame...the expanse of our distance...and the depth of our fall.

Let us lay here, just us two…and realize there are no others…that if we are to be touched, it will be by one another. Let us touch ourselves first to know our own touch…then touch each other to experience the difference. For your touch is what I seek.

Let us lie here in darkness and touch and retouch…let me touch your body that was once there for me to touch…while you touch my body…that was meant to be touched by you.

Touch me and test your hasty vows to never be touched by man again…help me and be forgiving of man…any man....all men. Teach me how to bring your love back from the dead…and as you have touched woman...touch me, for it was originally meant to be.

For I will still love you...in whatever form you take...for you... woman...any woman and all women are the object of my new journey and my new desire to love...for you are still woman.

We cannot regulate our love ever again...it has been set free...and it knows no bounds now that I can see...now that I can feel...now that I can learn.

For the love and the desires that now embrace us...will never again be bound by society...by the will of others...by ancient interpreters...or bound by race, creed or color. For we both have strayed from the path of God.

I will not judge you for I am not fully aware of your imagined needs and desires. But love will return in time to those who love, and love will reach out to those whom we love...and love will continue to grow from man to woman...and from woman to man. For all love is nourished by God and will lack for nothing. For the emotion of love was not your first emotion as you were taught that you...woman...had committed some serious crime and that you and your kind had caused us to be born in sin...that you were the source of evil and of man's downfall...the cause of the original sin.

How ridiculous!

You were draped in the cloak of shame and despair...hostility and anger. You were the cause...you were the blame. It was your crime...your cloak...your first garment...but it was placed there by man not God...and you were dressed as a bride of sin from the beginning.

And man draped this garment on your body as a cast...a cast that molded the blame and the reason for man's life of hardship to every fold of your body.

Fear and confusion occupied the minds of the Adams and Eves throughout the world...and love had not yet been born...nor spoken of in most religious structures..

And you have attached your mind to this guilt and you have drawn the cloak of blame even closer to your body...and some of you have accepted a guilt...a shame...and your evilness...and you have allowed it to be passed on by ancient men with ancient minds...and you assisted by programming your daughters and your daughter's daughters to accept the inevitable domination of man over woman.

You have accepted this false cloak of blame designed and tailored by ancient men with ancient minds. Men that have designed the ignorance of your future...men that have designed the weight of the guilt that you bear...on legs insufficient to the task.

Forced to bear a guilt before sharing the love of man...convinced that your pain would be in giving birth...as a punishment for some imaginary crime...a crime told by ancient men to those willing to accept.

In your acceptance and ignorance you realized that you could never hear the screams of the animals as they gave birth in silence and wondered why.

And you wondered why you were thought unclean as you bled giving life and were further perplexed that the blood of animals was not considered unclean as man dug in with his bare hands to deliver a new racing foal or a championship dog.

Man did not send the bleeding prize cow to a hut for unclean cows when it bled. Man did not fear unclean blood as he sat in the corner of the stall eating his lunch after having delivered a prize stallion. Only the blood of woman was unclean. Only you...woman any woman...all women...would accept this ridiculous disrespect for giving life.

And while some religions would drink the blood of a new born calf...woman...any woman...all are unclean.

Leviticus 12: 2 - "If a woman hath conceived seed , and born a man child : then she shall be unclean for 7 days;"

And in *Leviticus 12: 5- "But if she bear a maid child, then she shall be unclean for two weeks."*

And in *Leviticus 12: 6- "And when the days of her purifying are fulfilled, for a son, or a daughter, she shall bring a lamb of the first year for a burnt offering, and a young pigeon or a turtle dove, for a sin offering, unto the door of the congregation, unto the priest.*

And even then your conceivement of life was a sin only relieved by a sin offering to a priest.

And in your acceptance, you have sent logic and knowledge of the tree of life to the bowels of the earth... for it is obvious that no woman ate from the tree of knowledge...and that no man took a bite...for our ability to communicate with God has been delegated to ancient men with ancient minds.

For it is obvious that man and woman...woman and man...had eaten from the tree of man's ignorance and guilt...and the seeds are still lodged in our throats.

Lodged there by ignorance as we dare to contemplate the beginning of man...the beginning of the universe...life after death...and where we will sit in the heavens above. But ancient man with ancient minds gave love and respect for you...woman...any woman...all women...a minor role, if any role at all.

For had we known love before guilt... compassion before punishment...and forgiveness before condemnation, we would never have abandoned love for each other...we would never have substituted woman for the teachings of ancient man with ancient minds.

It is far more important to prove that we can love again. That is the true challenge. For we cannot save the world until we love again…you and I...man and woman…woman and man.

We must at all cost close this gap…you and I… for it must become a ramp…a crossing for all that vow to never love again. A ramp that will lead one to a better understanding and interpretation of our need to love.

A ramp that will not allow ignorance to tread its path...a ramp that will resist the passage of disrespect and dishonor...a ramp that will not give passage to evil. For this ramp between us must only carry our love… back and forth…forth and back.

14
NEW RULES OF LOVE

he complexities of who we love should never bind us again, for these boundaries have limited our ability to love.

For years and in many countries man has has again and again set the rules for love contrary to the essence of God and man, and has allowed you to love, but not question…to be questioned, but not loved…to not be loved and still be questioned. He has set impossible task for you to display your love…and has set boundaries for his return display. While you must love, honor and respect man with no boundaries, some men set boundaries for his display of love for you.

Man has dictated such a rift between us that we both are confused about how much to love...who to love…when to love…and whether to love at all. Where God called for you to love all men…man has caused you to love few...if any at all.

Man...who has never been to the deepest portion of the ocean, and still cannot tell us what lies in these shallow depths, would have us believe that he has knowledge of the vast universe and is able to tell us the mystery of the beginning of life. Man who cannot agree on the known tenets of love, respect and understanding, dares to interpret the creator.

Ancient men, who earlier cursed women who bore twins, believed that she must have lain with two men, but yet these men would profess knowledge of the beginning of humanity.

Ancient men with ancient minds will say that man and woman were formed from clay or dust as the breath of God blew over. He will then say that Eve was taken from the rib of man as she lay sleeping...and whatever myth or legend that comes to mind.

Mix and match...match and mix as man selects from the hundreds of ancient stories of man's beginning.

It is time for ancient men with ancient minds to leave the initial mysteries of God alone and to concentrate on the mysteries of love and respect. For we will never know God...your God...my God...our God... until we decipher the mysteries of love and respect...for they are the most attainable goals placed before us and are the first step towards the directives of our God.

As I come to you...I ask that you not resent my phallic appendage...for it was given to me by God... and only represents a small portion of my ability to express my love for you.

In this new loving of man and woman...of woman and man...it is the instrument that will continue to bind...for it is the instrument of creation...it is the instrument to probe and bring forth life...doing God's bidding...although in the past it has been the undoing of God's design.

It is one of the instruments, along with the mind and the heart, that binds man to woman and woman to man.

Can we return to a new concept of a garden as we once were....nude…side-by-side…skin-to skin…breast-to-breast..loin-to-loin…arms entwined? Can you hate me as much lying here beside me? Is there a greater hate than when we are clothed? Do you feel more vulnerable? Will you...woman...seek to abstract revenge for past injustices against those that went before us…and will you take the blame for those of you that have been unjust to man?

We are a unit…incomplete without each other and useless when unconnected…disorientated when not in sync...not capable of producing quality life when divided by anger...distrust or fear.

We will redeem our unfulfilled lives and we will unmask our need for each other. For as others search for holy ground we will declare where we stand as the holiest of ground, for it is the base of man and woman...woman and man, and this base was provided for by my God...your God...and our God.

I am not from Mars and you are not from Venus…for life has not been found on either of these planets…and together we represent life. I have not been to the mountain tops nor have I sat in isolation from you woman...spending my time talking to burning bushes or extraterrestrials, for I have come from you and out of your womb...and will spend my time trying to stay connected to you as God planned.

For we did not create our life and have no knowledge of how we came to be...where we came from or why. But I do know that you...woman...are the chamber of our birth, created by the insertion of man...and to me one is no greater than the other.

In the various attempts to explain the reasons for the creation of man and woman or the relationship to a God, many religions, BCE, CE and AD, left the portrayal to ancient men with ancient minds or to self appointed oracles or prophets that existed in isolation.

Mere man, affected by the heat of the desert or the cold of the mountain caves...affected by the darkness of the forest or the vastness of the wilderness...man affected by the solitude and the hallucinations of his mind, imagined that he heard the voice of God.

Traveling North...East...South...and West... many men heard voices...but they never heard the voice of woman and so she was excluded from the word.

Would a scientist attempt to study science by excluding 1/2 of the ingredient necessary for production? These ancient men, void of original ideas, mixed and matched various beliefs, pagan rituals and superstitions and insisted that this was the word of God. How else would they have any value?

In one religion, man could be elevated to a God upon the performance of some deed of great merit. In another religion man was the servant of God.

And in yet another, man was the offspring of a God, sent to save man from man. Depending on the region and the religion...man was either subjected to being punished for seeking knowledge from the tree of life, disobeying God, seeking to become like God, or for his desire to be immortal and knowledgeable like God.

God, being a jealous God, would have none of this according to ancient men with ancient minds. They were appalled that anyone would then challenge their interpretations and so designated that those who did not conform to their vision is guilty of questioning God.

These religions had designated a God for you and I…man and woman…and for woman and man. And it was this jealous God that punished humanity for seeking youth, knowledge and immortality.

This desire for attributes that are today much sought after, is attributed to the cause of mans fall from grace, burdening woman with a painful birth, and all other retributions that forever burden man and woman…woman and man. The religious interpretations by ancient men with ancient minds and their beliefs now become the causes of never ending conflicts and wars against all non-believers.

They have created a jealous God indeed.

I will not be party to attempts to claim the site of the birth of man and woman...woman and man, as this attempt lies at the root of mankind's conflict.

Can one know where gold or silver was first found? Does man know where the first wind blew? Does man know where the first leaf fell to the ground?

It is foolish to accept any knowledge of these things and even more foolish to take the life of those that do not agree.

It is foolish to give the power of interpretation to any race creed or color for they would play at being God. In their desire to confuse and control they will exclude the attempts by God to show a common thread that has ran through humanity from the beginning of time. They will deny the existence of the similarities of man's efforts to understand that which man and woman will never understand.

Ancient men with ancient minds will preach their dogmas based on the fear of a God that will punish those that do not blindly follow their interpretation of God. All religions based on this fear will distort historical information and will restrict information to serve their needs. They will deny that previous religions had also claimed a crucified earthly God or that they had taken license with these mythical tales.

What of Thulis of Egypt in 1700 BC who was said to have been crucified, buried, rose again, ascended to heaven and returned to benefit humanity?

What of Krishna of India 1220 B.C, said to be born of a virgin, visited by shepherds, wise men and angels who sang.

Krishna was credited with the parting of the River Jumna to allow an escape path and spent time in the desert before being baptized in the River Ganges. Krishna is documented as being suspended on a cross or a tree with pierced holes in his feet. His followers were assured that he would return to always be with them, and on his death he was anointed with oil by women.

And there are hundreds of other plagiarisms done in the name of religion. Mix and match...match and mix... but never allow the doctrine of respect and love for women to divert from the teachings of ancient men with ancient minds.

What of Atys of Phrygia in 1170 B.C who was documented as being suspended on a tree, crucified, buried and rose, from a state of death?

What of Thammuz of Syria in 1160 BC who was immortalized in poem as being the one to trust in as he rose from the dead to atone for the sins of man?

What of Hesus of the Celtic Druids in 834 B.C who was reported crucified with the symbols of the lamb at his side which represented innocence and was used as a sacrifice for the sins of man?

What of Bali of Orissa in 725 B.C. whose followers believed that he was crucified and included in a "Father, Son and Holy Ghost trinity and was known as the "Crucified Redeemer"?

And what of Mithra of Persia in 600 BC whose myth has it that he was slain and placed on a cross to

It is believed that Mithra was born of a virgin in a stable around December 25 on the Julian Calendar. Myth has it that he was visited by shepherds who brought gifts and he was depicted with a halo around his head and had a last supper before returning to the heavens only to return to earth to raise the dead before deciding who would go to heaven and who would go to hell. Mithra's days were celebrated by sacraments of bread and wine and utilized bells, candles, incense and holy water in ceremonies in honor of Mithra's last meal on earth.

Would we continue to follow those who have distorted history and claimed their beliefs as original?

It is foolish to believe that ancient men with ancient minds can lead us, when they have never learned to follow God! It is foolish to believe that God, in all of God's wisdom, would not create a home land for other races equally seeking to escape from the oppression of others. It is up to you and I...man and woman...woman and man to create a garden of our own, free from ancient men with ancient minds who do not share the pleasures or the reasons for our unity.

Where ancient men with ancient minds have created a God of vengeance, we will create a God of forgiveness. Where ancient men with ancient minds attempted to restrict us from hearing the voice of God other than through them, we will hear the voice of God whether waking or sleeping. For trying to stop the world from hearing the word of God is like attempting to stop the rising of the sun.

Where they have interpreted the written words of ancient men with ancient minds, we will interpret the feeling of God for the good of us all.

Come...love me...mentally...physically and spiritually. Let our minds and our bodies flow with the importance of this new journey with a new purpose which is to reunite you and I...man and woman... woman and man.

Will you respond to my touch and can I respond to yours? Will our response be an honest response...or will it carry the baggage of years gone by...with memories of lies...disrespect...and of violence? Will you realize that God created this need for each other...this desire to make love...this desire to touch and to love...and to reproduce? All emotions instilled by God.

With this touch...we will ignite and unite and settle our differences...undisturbed by religious indoctrination and interpretations of ancient men that have never known this fire...the fire whose embers were placed in us by God. For if they lack the love or the desire for you....woman...why would God allow them any say in the affairs of the heart?

I do not wish to make love to you as a challenge to my manhood...for there is something of far greater importance to prove. It is far more important to prove that we can love again. That is the true challenge. For we cannot save the world until we love again...you and I...man and woman...woman and man.

The goal to save and unite all men and women and women and men will never be achieved...but it is a goal that we must aim for. For does man not spend billions to attempt to communicate with outer space...to listen for the faintest sounds on billion dollar equipment...to incorporate the latest technology...to promote the importance of outer space travel and the conquering of space? But yet these efforts will not be commanded to communicate with God's creation... Woman.

It is you and I...man and woman...woman and man that must now begin to explore our existence. We must, at all cost, close this gap which is as vast as the universe, for our love must become a ramp...a crossing for all that had vowed to never love again. A ramp that will lead one to a better understanding and interpretation of our need to love.

A ramp that will not allow ignorance to tread it's path...a ramp that will resist the passage of disrespect and dishonor...a ramp that will not give passage to evil. For this ramp between us must only carry our love... back and forth...forth and back but not backward.

Is that surprise I see in your face? Do you now realize that I wish not to dominate but to communicate.. to share in the give and take of love and to share our life and our love for generations to come? Secure as we soar to heights that only we can soar together...secure as we soar to heights that one can only reach in the hands of God. For separate and without each other we will continue to plummet to the depths of the earth.

You must step out of the darkness…for I know that you will have much to say to me. I know that I… man…have made it hard for you to speak…and now with that license you know not where to begin.

Man has controlled you…not controlled you…. and at times has left you uncontrollable. Man has expressed his blindness to you and your virtues and has caused you to be blinded by his blindness.

And as the blind leads the blind…we stumble in the wrong direction…in darkness…denying sight for generations to come.

15
SURROGATE LOVER

Excuse me dear creature of the night, why do you lurk in this dark and unfriendly place?

Why do you reach out and touch only strangers…beckoning them to come with you? When you called to me, did you know that I was a stranger only seeking to understand?

I have been watching you…and I know that you feel that you have some purpose here…as you brazenly parade your wares for all to see. You say that I talk too much…and that I should move on…as we have no business you and I…man and woman…woman and man.

You say that you are not here for your health, and that I truly believe…for you and your dark and darker promises are not here for the health of anyone… for they are the expression of the bad health that exists between you and I...man and woman…woman and man.

But if you feel that you must be here, then here you must be…for you have decided to live your life as you see fit...driven to this solitary decision by misunderstanding and despair.

But I must live my life according to God...and that life is with you...as man and woman...woman and man.

I know that you feel that your life is yours and yours alone...as is death when you die. But for now... while you will allow...and before you flee...I will reach out to you.

I notice the fear in your eyes as you talk to me... a stranger. How complex it must be to fear man, but yet...for a price...you will bare your life giving chamber as you act out your farce of love...never knowing whether man will react to your love with love, or with violence.

I notice your fear as you bear your life giving chamber in woman's most vulnerable position...prone... submissive and open.

Never knowing whether man's response will be to make love to you...as you play at loving him...or will he play at hate...for your loving to play at love.

How driven and confused you must be to face this challenge...this ordeal...this trial...every night., acting out a self inflicted punishment for ancient man's accusation against woman...any woman...all women.

I think of the women that dread this act with their known mate...with the father of their children... with controllers of their fate...but yet you perform this act with complete strangers.

Come my love...you self-appointed surrogate of love...let me see what qualifies you to replace wives and lovers of this world with your second-class service.

Let me see why men turn to you for love's expression...in spite of the fact that they know that you are not capable of truly loving them...in spite of the fact that they will be heaped with scorn and condemned by their families...their society and by God. A God that is blamed for this contradiction.

For love is not really what you offer...what you really offer is insertion and release. For this...and this alone is what man receives when he partakes of your services.

Be it known that man will enter woman...man... children...animals...and even himself when he can. While women will be inserted by man... woman... children...animals...with vegetables...and by her own hand, so strong is this desire to stimulate woman's reproductive chamber of life...given to her by God.

Man and woman will always respond to insertion and release. In any race...any age...any color...any religion...and at anytime.

Release and insertion can and will change the direction of our lives...whether by force or by consent, for after insertion and release...we will never be the same. For if I love you with consent...I will always love you with consent...but if man makes love to you by force, then man will always make love by force.

You…daughter of darkness…this is what you offer…insertion and release…all for a price. But who ends up paying that price? The stranger who finds you lurking here in the dark or you, the woman that lurks...or the whole world that is plunged into darkness by your act?

For God did not put a price on love…or on the expressions of love. Who will now pay for your desperate expression of love…this insertion and release…this instant gratification that will forever extract an incalculable debt from the world?

For when men leave you...the Daughter of Darkness...they are forever tainted by this type of love. For it not only stains the garments and is wasted on the soil…but it stains the mind and the soul and the true expression of love will forever be changed.

I see that men of every country brazenly seek you out…you women who have traveled throughout history and throughout the world...always lurking in the dark passages, as much a part of history as history itself.

You lurk in the shadows of Europe...North America...Asia...and Africa.

You lurk on the throne of power and under the feet of power…but you lurk all the same.

You lurked in the days of Cleopatra and you lurk in the days of the modern day madams...and you will probably always lurk...unless we exchange our love and respect for each other.

241

You lurked in secret places accessed only by secret passwords...but today you blatantly advertise on public media with preferences, ages and price. While you lurk in the dark passages of the world...others lurk in the spotlight of high society...others lurk as the girl next door...others lurk as the woman of our foolish dreams...and others lurk as victims waiting to be victimized.

For your type of love has been accepted at all levels of our society.

You have engaged in your profession for love... for loss of love...for economics...for politics...for survival...for loneliness...for despair...for necessity...for fear, and for misunderstanding God's goal for your love and the dispensing of that love.

Monetary gains are not what you seek and will never fill your real needs. In your desire to be loved... you sell undesirable love. In your desire to be loved... you...woman...sell an expression of love and then pass the rewards to someone who will express a form of love to you. How totally confusing!

How confusing to seek someone that will only express love to you if you sell your love to a stranger. How confusing to then expect that this love...will free you to love freely.

How confusing to know that false love can be expressed in many varied ways...but true love only knows the way of truth.

Where did you learn the performance of love? When did it become a sham? Where is it written that the act of love is not the act of love…but merely an act?

Are you the only one that carries the shame of a whore? Must this title only be bestowed to your sisters of the night that lurk in dark places? Are you the only one with a motive for you expressions of love? What of those that marry for money…for title…for position...for escape...for revenge..for security...for excitement...for the children...for fear?

Motives other than love are still motives…and links you and your sisters of the night...closer and closer...closer in thought…closer in deed…and closer in results.

For in the end…motives other than love will destroy us all.

We must all step into a different light…a light that will uncover our deception to each other…for we men lurk also in the dark...and our motives…when not motives of true love…link us all into the same darkness that we have driven you into.

You must step out of the darkness…for I know that you will have much to say to me. I know that I… man...have made it hard for you to speak…and now with that license you know not where to begin.

Man has controlled you…not controlled you.... and at times has left you uncontrollable.

Man has expressed his blindness to you and your virtues and has caused you to be blinded by his blindness. And as the blind leads the blind...we stumble in the wrong direction...in darkness...denying sight for generations to come.

But now this injustice must be registered and placed aside...as history should be. For man's interpretation of history has caused history to be interpreted by man...for man...and to the detriment of man...any man...all men...and to the world.

Not to be forgotten...but not to be re-lived.

As the Jews must place aside their mistreatment...as the Arabs must place aside their mistreatment...as the Blacks must place aside their mistreatment, as the Whites must place aside their mistreatment...as the Indians must place aside their mistreatment, as the Asians must place aside their mistreatment, and on and on and on and on.

For this energy of hatred and revenge cannot truly coexist within a heart that needs more room for love. For this hatred will not allow the heart to expand and absorb new love...for the walls of the heart will remain hardened and restricted.

This energy for hatred and revenge will not step willingly aside to allow for healing...teaching...and loving. And as cancer will not willingly step aside to allow healthy cells to grow...neither will hatred and revenge allow love to grow within the same chamber of our soul.

You woman...and I...man...must set aside our injustices to each other. For we must not be bounty hunters of the past...as the reward is too low and the price we pay...to high. For if we live in a failed past.... it will surely destroy us...you and I...man and woman.. woman and man...our children and their children.

PART III

THE NEED IS
GREATER
THAN EVER

When man returned from his wars…you cheered him…when you should have turned from him in shame…for he had just returned from killing…from raping…from torturing…and from enslaving your sisters and your sister's children in a foreign land.

And when the winds of war died for a moment...you wondered why you were murdered... raped...tortured…and enslaved...in your country...in your streets...in your home…and in your bed.

16
HEAD IN THE SAND

our life has been such confusion…it is truly the marvel of this world which no man made creations can equal. There are not seven wonders of the world…there is only one…you…woman.

Man cannot re-create the strength required for you to survive the onslaught of man on your person… on your mind…and on your body. God must have known the pressures that you…the mother of all…the giver of life, would have to bear to fulfill God's concept of man and woman...woman and man. And God, in all God's wisdom, would know that man would be man, while trying to be God.

You did not become extinct like the dinosaur… you did not disappear...even though your environment changed…placing your very existence in jeopardy everyday of your life.

It proves the strength that God put in the creation of you...woman...the bearer of life...with such a strong will to survive.

God knew that man, in his desire to be God, would test your sanity and your strength for this unimaginable task placed on you and that you would need inhuman strength to survive and continue to survive.

But I now notice the strain of these demands. They are becoming greater...more distressing...and more mutated into something that we no longer can control...no longer live with or allow to live any longer.

You are not blameless...for you have occasionally played an equal role in this masquerade... this false loving...this fiction of love. Crimes have been committed and permitted in your name...in your honor...in your stead and in your heart.

When you...a witness...should have spoken out and been a member of the jury or the judge...at times you chose to act as an innocent bystander...a spectator...a fan. You were content to stand in the shadows of man's injustice to man...while he initiated and practiced the eventual crimes that he would re-visit upon you.

The rape of the enemy's woman...would be practice for raping you...the rape of the children of the enemy would be the rape of your children one day.

The violence practiced on another race would one day be practiced on you.

The control of other races and disrespect for their rights would be perfected on them and used on you. And as you consider yourself blameless...the world knows that you are one-half the blame.

You made the attainment of a seat on the throne your goal…you became a symbol of man's power when you should have been the source of his wisdom...his compassion…his love.

In the frustration of your interpretation of your role…you were taught to not know man until you were 16…and by then you were the proud possessor of 16 years of ignorance and confusion as to your role with man.

You did not know yourself…as emotions were yet to be discovered…and you did not know man. Instead of bringing knowledge...awareness and hope many brought fear...anxiety...gullibility and inexperience.

You were then expected to come to his bed... honor and obey…worship and suffer…bear and raise... live and die…but there was no guarantee of love... protection or even respect.

If you were to know man before your husband... you were soiled. If you were to know your husband before marriage...you were easy. If you were raped by another...you were rejected and deemed as a shame and embarrassment to the family.

You were the cause and the blame for every action and reaction.

You could not win…you could not win…you could not win.

If man were to know woman before his wife it was practice. If man were to know his wife before marriage...it was his right. If man raped...you asked for it. Man was not the cause or blame for any action or reaction.

He could not lose...he could not lose...he could not lose.

You were ordered to love and respect...honor and obey before you knew him...but yet you had not become a friend.

He was not required to love or respect...or honor or obey and you envied those that had found this loving relationship with man. But you were convinced that the choice was still man's and the male jury was still out...and could be out for all the years of your life.

And when love did not flourish...the absence of a connection with your mate for life...floated in outer space...hoping to re-enter somewhere...sometime...in some form...in some life...but possibly disintegrating somewhere in outer space.

You woman...and your body...and the rewards thereof, were used to spur men on to acts of bravery... foolishness...cowardice...ignorance and murder. And when men returned from the countless and senseless wars...you honored him by force...but sometimes by choice.

When man returned from his wars...you cheered him...when you should have turned from him in shame...for he had just returned from killing...from raping...from torturing...and from enslaving your sisters and your sister's children in a foreign land.

And when the winds of war died for a moment...you wondered why women were murdered... raped...tortured...and enslaved in such alarming numbers. They have been murdered in their country...raped in their streets...enslaved in the homes and tortured in their beds.

You were first a child of God...then the property of your parents...and then the property of your husband. How confusing all of this must be.

You were blinded by the system that your sisters and your mothers...your grandmothers and your great grandmothers...your great-great grandmothers and their mothers...and their mother's mother allowed to flourish, grow and strengthen.

This same system had created dresses of racial injustice and war and it was now your turn to dress for the occasion. And you appeared on the stage dressed to suppress and to impress those that would deny you your basic rights.

The system that you helped strengthen as a member of the privileged class...or the beautiful class....or the wealthy class...or the educated class...or the ruling class...has come back in its idleness and boredom...to haunt you.

While you hid your head in the sand your sisters were being buried in the deeds of your leaders...your armies...your fathers...your brothers...your husbands...your sons...your lovers and your church. Deeds of hate...rape...violence...and war. And you... woman...in an act of patriotism, were asked to give forgiveness, and to condone or understand the most horrific deeds.

Some of you could take the system no longer and protested in the streets...frightening those still in the home...in the bedroom...and in the boardroom.

But others, with their head in the sand, and their rears exposed to the world..wiggled with joy at first when their rebellious sisters were jailed...beaten...and humiliated when they roamed the streets, giving protest to the living hell that you helped create.

Rather than join the fray...lending your strengths...you distanced yourself from the struggle and insisted that they should have stayed at home...safe in the arms of matrimony...with 2.0 children...the PTA...and a Search for a Tomorrow that would never come.

You then watched as your friends divorced and took lovers...some male...some female...and some took both.

Some black...some white...and some took one of each. Some went common-law...and some went to communes.

And as Madison Avenue and Hollywood discovered the economic value of your misery and frustration...they knew, as vultures knew, that your body and mind were dead and ready to be victims for their talons.

They invaded your home daily with the misery of married life...love life...and life in general. Along with the detergent commercials they showed you lust in the office...lust in the neighborhood...and lust in the church. They showed you incest...lies...infidelity... hysteria and criminality...all being sipped from crystal clear champagne glasses while you were sitting on plush couches in the living room or in cold water ghetto flats. They scripted the most exotic scenes of sexual release...and demanded that you compare the script with your release...and they moaned and groaned for hours it seemed...locked in the throes of a climax that you had never experienced...a climax that could not be matched in your mundane world...all locked in mini-series as your script of pain loomed larger than life.

A climax that John, Tom, George and Bill would never allow you to experience...while they scripted a scene for Antonio, Mark, Eric and Rock... with unreal creatures with their young breast pointing to the sky...with a waist that could be grasped by a single arm. Creatures with hair that flowed and spread over the silk sheets...with unblemished skin that shined and glistened...reflecting their sweat of passion. They squirmed and sought the approval of the camera, setting an unattainable goal of ecstasy for all.

And you both turned to each other and fantasized…and blotted out the reality of what you saw and what you felt…and the fantasy continued...on screen and off. And you became disenchanted as Hollywood showed you fire that would consume you and your ability to separate fact from fiction.

They exposed you to uncontrollable children... while showing your children how to be uncontrollable. They showed you values that had no value…while you denied value for those things with value.

And that evening you attempted to relive these dramas in real life…and became a spectator in your own home... unable to decipher between real life and TV life...and you became them…with a script written in hell.

You turned from the touch of man to the touch of a dial…and it showed you a life the same as yours but yet not yours…and you gloried in the fact that voyeurism allowed you to peer into the life of made for TV families.

And you spoke to them, this soap opera family that could not be made clean, and attempted to redirect their lives even though the script had already been written as you shouted out solutions to their scripted act, while your script was never completed…as you waited and watched others for half-hour episodes of artificial life...day in...and day out... "All the Days of your Life" as you "Search for Tomorrow" with "One Life to Live" without "All My Children."

"GOD
GRANT ME THE SERENITY
TO ACCEPT THINGS
I CANNOT CHANGE,
COURAGE
TO CHANGE THINGS I CAN,
AND
WISDOM
TO KNOW THE DIFFERENCE."

17
FOOTSTEPS OF PROTEST

 uddenly you found that you were 40…
and you complained of the elusiveness of
"The Big O…and so you read...studied...
and demanded more. More...more…more.

And the conflict built up within you sparked by
the media…by media that had the same conflicts
within, but found your frustrations as an inspiration
and income for theirs.

And suddenly, like the alliance of the United
Nations, some of you joined the streets of protest and
all hell broke loose. You beckoned others to come out
of the closest…for all the world to see…you bought
book after book on children…marriage…the
frustrations of children…the frustrations of marriage…
how to live alone…and how to live with more than one.

You exposed your life in the bedroom and in the
boardroom...you exposed your life in the ghetto and
barrio...you transposed the White House into the
outhouse…and no one knew the difference. It was time
to kiss and tell and kiss and sell. You commandeered
the media…the movie...and the bookstore, and you
demanded freedom_freedom for jobs...freedom for
equal pay...climaxes...oral sex...and more...more...more,
and you said it was your right and that it was long
overdue.

You wrote to Abby before you wrote to man…
and the ten short line answer formed the basis for your
response to a relationship in dire trouble and in need of
a library of solutions. Ten short lines…read between
commercials...ten short lines published daily. Ten short
lines on how to make your man love you…ten short
lines read between commercials...ten short lines on how
to leave your husband in ten short lines…ten short lines
on how to have an affair...with a younger man…with
an older man…with an older woman...with a younger
woman…with two men…or with three. And like the
church you were told to go and sin no more, as you
went and sinned some more.

And you wrote to advice columns writers and
their clones…while some of them divorced and failed
to follow their own advice. And the magazine sales sky
rocketed as you screamed for a 3 minute fix to
problems that God had prescribed the solution to
 thousands of years ago. And you screamed for help
from other Gurus.... and turned deaf to God's solution.
that was and is commercial free. And now you march…
and now you shout...and now you rail against man and
against woman…and against God. And in your anger
you take the life of your children...your husband and
yourself, as the strain of suppression takes it's toll on
you, the bearer of life. And you now compete with man
for a seat on death row as the bearer of life now
becomes the taker of life

You protest as man protested...with faces
twisted in anger…with faces twisted in hate…with
voices screaming obscenities…making the same
mistakes as man…as you follow in his footsteps of
ignorance.

Following his footsteps of mistake after mistake after mistake...following footsteps that will lead you further and further from God's plan for for you and I....man and woman...woman and man.

And your footsteps have led you to the place of despair...and you have caught up with man...for he reached there long before you...and as he left a troubled path...you too must follow.

For in the telling of the beginning of man and woman, you could not help but be confused...as ancient men...with ancient minds continued their confusion as they attempted to define the beginning of you and I...man and woman...woman and man.

****

And Adam had named all of the animals of the garden and sat in loneliness as he watched them mate and play with their off springs. He sat in silence and wondered why he had no one in the garden in his image. He confronted the animals one by one and found no compatibility with them in any way and he then returned to his resting place dropping his head into the palms of his hands in loneliness. At 24 he felt older for there was no joy in his life. He turned his head to the heavens and cried: "Every creature but I have a proper mate!" He listened in silence for a reason, but God did not answer.

Having heard the cry of Adam, God gathered the dust from the ground, except instead of using the pure fertile soil of the earth, God selected filth and sediment.

In an unexplainable act, God created Lilith as a demon that would plague mankind forever. Was God angry that Adam lusted after her flesh and that he was not satisfied with being the sole human creation of God?

When Adam attempted to lie with Lilith, she took offence to his requested missionary position, and insisted on being on top. Being told that she was the equal of man she demanded to know why she must submit to his request and said: "Why must I lie beneath you? For I am your equal and made from the earth the same as you. And we are both equal for we are both issued from dust and I will not submit to you."

And there was no peace between them.

****

Adam, being the stronger, was the first man that attempted to use force on a woman for sexual gratification, but Lilith invoked the magical name of God and this allowed her to escape by raising in the air.

Adam in his heightened sexual passion called out to God complaining that he had been deserted by this woman creature who had the audacity to make demands and to not completely comply with his wishes. "I have been deserted" he cried.

God too was angered and sent three angels, Senoy, Sansenoy and Samangelof (Senoi, Sansenoi and Sammangelof in some books) to fetch Lilith back. Lilith had joined other lascivious demons beside the Red Sea, where she had begun to bear demon children, beginning with 'Lilim' at the rate of more than 100 a day.

Upon the command to return to Adam immediately and to submit to his advances without complaint or face death by drowning, Lilith asked: "How can I return to Adam and submit to his wishes, as I have been given new duties by God?" She then convinced the three angels that she would not harm any circumcised boys if they displayed a sign. In Jewish tradition protection was sought against Lilith as she was seen as a threat to new borne male children as retaliation against Adam, and until a male child could receive circumcision in a Jewish house he was under threat of being fondled by Lilith.

To protect the child a circle was placed on the birth room with the names of the three angles inscribed or the name of Adam and Eve were written implying that the child was conceived under their protection.

The 2000 BC concept of Lilith is found throughout Babylonian-Assyrian history, on Sumerian tablets, in Greek history, Hebrew tradition and in the Bible. Lilith was credited in Talmudic tradition as being the possessor of many evils and was shown as a night creature because of the belief that she drains single men of their seed while sleeping on their back. She was accused in Jewish folklore of being a vampire-child killer and the symbol of sexual lust.

In Hellenistic belief, myth also has it that the daughters of Lilith were responsible for causing night emissions in men as they straddled them in missionary positions..

Lilith is credited as being the first wife of Adam and was described as being born of dust and or clay.

Eve was the second wife and was taken from the rib of Adam so that she would know, without a doubt, that she was not equal to the man.

And Eve, God's second attempt to supply the needs of Adam, also defiled the will of God by tempting Adam with the tree of knowledge. Then ancient men with ancient minds decided that all women were evil and the cause of the downfall of man...any man...all men. A myth brought to life to cause death.

****

And these ancient myths and legends are foisted on you and I...man and woman...woman and man.

It is small wonder that we are confused...it is obvious that we must discard myths and ancient concepts of others who are lying in their graves laughing at our acceptance of their ancient beliefs...believing that we have no choice but to accept these riddles of *theirhistory.*

Ancient myths and legends separated and allowed to only be discussed by ancient men with ancient minds...separated by them from fact and wrapped in cloths of black...never opened to challenges by anyone but one of their own kind. Truly a secret society...shrouded and insulated from the life of the ordinary man by a shield of defense to outside inquiries. Always at the ready to justify their roles as the go between between God. Always fearful that one day we will realize that we also can speak direct...making their robes and blessings useless.

It is time to abandon ancient men's concept of the word of God?

Ancient men with ancient minds would not for one moment discuss God with us, as they will declare that the mysteries of God are too complex for our simple minds...you and I...man and woman...woman and man...God's creation. For we are not the chosen people...someone else is.

For we do not deserve a holy land...someone else does...for God never speaks to us for we are not the chosen people. Is it not time that we abandon ancient men with ancient minds and allow the will of God to guide our lives?

Is it not time to acknowledge that the words of man are merely the words of man? Is it not time to ignore man's claim that God speaks to us through them and their self-appointed prophets?

It is time for me to acknowledge the will of God by loving you...woman...any woman...all women. It is time for me to find my own words from God...words that will foster respect...concern and love not only for you...woman...but for all humankind.

It is time to ignore the claims of ancient men with ancient minds that they have the books of God when they merely have the books of man. Man made books, scrolls and manuals that will continue to be how- to-manuals on perpetual hate and war between the races and sexes.

It is time to abandon the many religious books that are little more than histories of small regions that seek to become Gods in our lives. Regions that would limit the wonders of God to their small square miles.

For they have claimed the lives of too many, and will claim many more.

It is time to acknowledge that the word of God can well be heard by man and woman...woman and man. It is time to realize that God's communication with us will be as the sound of a tree falling in the forest with no one to hear it.

When...man and woman...woman and man are where God wants them to be, they will hear the word.

It is time that we now feel the will of God for it is not a word...it is a way of life. It is not a burning bush...it is our burning soul. It is not a scroll nor a parchment...it is our ability to love and to respect each other...it is not an order, but a matter of our mind and the muscle of our heart.

It is not time spent on our knees...but on our feet. It is not time spent bowing our heads...but time to hold them high. It is not accepting blame for original sin...but accepting original love. It is not stories to fear God's wrath, but to accept God's love. It is time to stop accepting the confusing thoughts of man as he interprets dreams as reality and reality as dreams…when he interprets illusions as signs from God and the mysteries of nature as signs of God's displeasure.

Thunder is no longer the sound of God's displeasure...fire is no longer the punishment for sin... lightning no longer strikes only the wicked...lust no longer is punished by blindness...and woman is not the cause of man's misfortune.

It is time to be released from the spell of vain and swelling bombastic animated speakers who appeal to our concept of theatre...speakers who practice in front of home mirrors with wordy speeches and animated rhetoric. It is time to turn off religious orators who stand on elevated platforms decorated with opulence, pomp and circumstance.

Men who follow the drama of Greek theatre and are loud...sing-song.and repetitious. They then bombard you with jokes as stand-up comedians. Men seeking listeners and applauders...but needing contributors most of all. Men who shout and contort...but allow no discussion.

Would any school teach this way?

It is not time to continue to let man guide you and I to God...but it is time for you and I to guide man and woman to God.

It is time to turn from man and turn to God.

They will condemn this writing as they will condemn all stimulants of thought...they will condemn this writing as they condemn all processes of freedom... they will condemn this book as they condemn all things that do not exalt them and their chosen profession.

They will ask for blind faith and a blind belief in their conclusions.

They will label your questioning of them, as a questioning of God...and some of you will accept and withdraw the use of your mind which was given to you by God.

And they will continue as ancient men with ancient minds as they have too much invested to turn back now as they seek the reverence of a God here on earth...knowing full well that their path is not the path of God.

18
THE EDGE OF THE CLIFF

nd now that we both at last stand side by side at the edge of the cliff...do we jump together or do we pull back.

Do you pull back...letting man plunge to his death by himself? For if you do you must surely follow. Or do we grasp each other and pull back together, pulling back all of humankind at one time.

Do we finally turn our ears once again to the voice of your God...my God...our God?

Only God would allow us to fail so badly and allow a second chance...a third chance and more.

I have stopped here at the edge of the cliff...for I see the fall of man if I do not stop and appeal to you. I have stopped here at the edge of the cliff, praying to see you stop also.

I have stopped here at the edge of the cliff so that we will plunge no farther. I have stopped at the edge of the cliff so that together we can see that there is no hope for us apart...divided...and un-united.

At this site we must change hostility to friendship…despair to hope…indifference to concern and tolerance to love. I say that you are as qualified as man to share the lead...to instruct…to love...and I welcome you.

Man has held you back…and you have held yourself back…and in doing so we both have contributed to holding back the world.

We are both guilty...so let us start this love affair anew…as we attempt to correct the injustices committed by both of us…injustices against each other and against the world

Let us start anew as we restore our ability to love…you and I…man and woman…woman and man.

Let the interpreters of the holy books continue to interpret for their personal power…let them continue to act as prophets...messengers... priest…and holy men... along with their self-imposed titles given to them, not by God, but given to them by a council of men.

They have chosen this mantle as a profession.... as a job...as an occupation as a source of income and a source of power, feeling that if you question them...you question God.

Maybe one day others will, as too much of a good thing must come to an end. For they know no limits to their power and will one day over reach their limits as they seek the autonomy of God.

Time will continue to tell.

Let them continue to sit in little rooms listening to your sinful confessions…let them wave their hands and say go and sin no more…let them find others to bow down to them…let them find others to kiss their rings and their hands and their feet…let them find others to sell all and give to them, while they sell nothing and keep all.

Let them continue to dress in robes of gold or suits of silk…let them feel the need for security… bodyguards…bulletproof glass and isolation from everyday man and woman.

For they read their ancient books and decree that you must serve them and God with the same reverence. In their confusion they regard all men and women as less instead of more…and decree their life or death as they see fit.

Let them change the history of religion to justify their slaughters as acts decreed by God. Let them continue to convince others that the way to God…my God…your God…our God…is through them.

Let them live with the wars that they, in their interpretation of God's word, have caused…years of war…years of deaths…and years of despair.

Let them write and mouth peace process after peace process…knowing full well that there will be none.

And they are not done yet.

They will continue to fight and maim…and judge and kill…all in the name of God.

They will find you guilty as God will surely find them guilty…but their punishment will be unbearable as in their supreme ignorance they fear not God or the wrath of God….as they play at God's role.

They will condemn this writing as they will condemn all stimulants of thought…they will condemn this writing as they condemn all processes of freedom… they will condemn this book as they condemn all things that do not exalt them and their chosen profession.

They have too much invested as they seek the reverence of a God here on earth…knowing full well that their path is not the path of God.

For ancient men with ancient thoughts believe that in your faith one should be humble while they are bold…that attempts at reason are interpreted as arrogance and are barbarous and sacrilegious. Ancient man demands that one must not give in to the pride of inquiry, but accept what ancient men with ancient minds say without deflection

Knowing full well that they appear to be the true none believers as they appear to be unmindful of God's vengeance...as they attempt to share God's throne.

For God did not say bow down to man...or kiss his hand...or kiss his feet for fear that ancient men could bring down the wrath of God.

And God did not ask for the ceremony of worship that has been taken to the highest form of theatre with lights, action and camera.

These innovations are the whims and fancy of ancient men....in ancient garb and now modern man in modern garb...all seeking comfort in modern times as ancient men for modern times.

God like in authority...but to be pitied in reality, as uneasily they attempt to wear God's crown.

My dreams have monsters....my dreams have visions...my dreams allow me to travel to the stars. My dreams attempt to consume me with fire...my dreams hear voices...my dreams show me visions of things to come...my dreams give me knowledge of all things. My dreams are on mountain tops...my dreams take place in the center of the earth...my dreams allow me to sit at the right hand of God.

But although my dreams seem as real as reality...my dreams are but my dreams. My dreams will not start a new religion. My dreams are separated by me from heavenly visitations...by nocturnal visions... but yet pondered upon and not totally dismissed. But eventually I file these dreams away and proceed to prepare my breakfast...as I will feed the me that exists in this world today. For I will somehow separate some of my dreams from my consciousness, not really sure which is which.

But I will not bring my tormented dreams to our world...and interpret them as visits from either demons...prophets or Gods.

For what I dream at night will stay in that realm...for there I am separated from you .

But ancient man without the comfort of you...woman...all women...any woman, will bring his dreams back to a male world as a visit and direction from his God or his demons...and will declare that the message is for the whole world.

In my dreams I sometimes suffer states of delusions and imagine power or weaknesses that are only temporary...I see visions that are unexplainable and beyond my comprehension. In my dreams I sometimes escape from the grasp of demons and other fire breathing creatures to terrible to imagine.

At night I run races never won...fall from cliffs, but never contact ragged rocks that would cradle my broken lifeless remains...I pass through fires that scorch and threaten to consume, but never do...I encounter demons that chase, and never catch, but leave me sweating and calling out in vain. All are but dreams that chase me back to the dawn of a new day where I am safe until I dream again, as God lets morning come, and releases me from my terror... seemingly as a warning of terrible things to come.

Ancient man brought these dreams back into his waking life...dreaming of visitations from Gods and demons, not knowing which to fear, love, obey... or proclaim as a new religion.

Not knowing whether it was the voice of God or the voice of dreams...but recalling that the visions filled him with fear...causing him to call out...to scream...to cry...to tremble...to draw into forms of embryos...and to run and run and run...while talons scratched at his flesh no matter how fast he ran.

Voices and dreams that caused the sweat to pour and the heart to pound...voices that caused ancient men with ancient minds to draw into corners of the bed, or the darkness of the cave or attempt to hide in the wilderness. Voices that made his skin burn and caused his muscles to tense...voices that would not go away. Voices that today are heard by many tormented addicts and those with mental illness. For those of today that hear voices of God would be prophets in ancient times.

Some heard voices and walked into the night...some heard voices as The Son of Sam...some heard voices that said jump...burn...kill...maim...take your life...take a life...or two or three or all the members of your family. Some were influenced by imagined voices of evil, but convinced themselves that these were the voice of God. Ancient man, wanting to be God, always heard the voice of God announcing him as the prophet or as the bearer of the news of the coming of the prophet or even that he was God!

The voice of God...never to the poets...never to the artist...never to the intellectuals...never to the masses and never...never...never to a woman...any woman...all women. The voice of God...never in the market place...never on a crowded street...never with a witness...always in the bush...or from a tree...or from a rock or from a mountain cave.

God...whose voice would know no bounds, is bound by ancient men with ancient minds.

God, whose voice is able to come to us all...is limited by those that profess that God only speaks to them in isolation.

From these isolations the word of God is carried to the battlefield by these ancient men with ancient minds.

The path to understanding the will of the creator can not be found on these battlefields of religious wars...for the price is too dear.

There are those who have the strength and the awareness of God within our souls that will stop at the gates of this madness...and realize that enough is enough and it must be you and I...man and woman... woman and man.

For we must withdraw and repair to our original cave to reunite...while the battle for the throne of God rages among the tribes...for it is only a battle between tribes and not between right and wrong or good or evil. A tribe in the North...a tribe in the West...a tribe in the South...and a tribe in the East. It is their conflict but it threatens to consume us all.

It is time that you and I...man and woman... woman and man...take note of the history of man... the confusion of interpretation...the history of misinformation...the violence to control our belief in God...your God...my God...our God.

We must at last stand back from this unlicensed use of our mind...while disenfranchising the use of our soul. We must begin to really see where the conflict lies. For it is not in God's plan that we continue to shop for religious beliefs...destroying the shopper as we encounter them.

Most of the world believe in one God...and probably has since the beginning of time...as history records the numerous attempts of man to accept monotheism as far back as 1385 BC when man looked to the Sun God in Egypt and worshipped it symbolic of the one true God and before.

Many religions have recorded attempts to define God...many have produced the models promoted today as original...many have recorded lost and found books of their religious scriptures.

But you and I...man and woman...woman and man must begin to stand together...side by side... facing the unknown together. We will move forward together...making our own decisions about the journey.

All humans share a belief in a creator...but some hear voices of war as they choose which creator to acknowledge. Some walk their personal path to God...while stretching out their hands in peace...while others walk with weapons of destruction...reaching out to inflict punishment while declaring that they and they alone know the path to God.

The choice of a belief in God is a personal choice…as is the journey to the top of a mountain. For in this journey no two footsteps will fall in the exact same place…but yet we can arrive at the summit of the mountain in peace…but yet appreciate the separate paths that we take.

If one believes in the power of God…then who would be better to enlighten the lost and misguided than God…rather than for man to do it with war? And if there is any validity to the claim that "vengeance is mine saith the Lord" then when did vengeance become the tool of man? God is a name selected…as humans attempt to identify the creator of their world and their existence. A name that is called to communicate with this creator. A name that should be freely chosen and freely called by you and I…man and woman…woman and man...without the fear of death at the hands of man.

For we are still in a process of evolutionism beginning with our stages of creationism. We are a product of naturalism and share a belief in intelligent design. We cover all bases as we attempt to understand that which cannot be scientifically proven. In our faith some can be convinced to have faith in the faith of others. The truth is we exist therefore we are but we may never know the reason why or how.

But by the grace of our creator, we will emerge unscathed...ready to live in peace and harmony...you and I...man and woman...woman and man...ever thankful for our creation.

☯

19
BINDING FORCE OF FRIENDSHIP

 say that you are as qualified as man to lead and instruct…and that you must acknowledge the fact that you are equally to blame for the woes of the world.

Steps were taken by both to create this distance between us…steps by man…and steps by woman. Admit it so that we can begin again.

Man has by force…held you back…and you by cunning…convenience or ignorance have held yourself back…and in doing so we have both held back the world.

Will ancient men with ancient minds not continue to involve us in war after war…religion after religion…God search after God search…modification after modification…revision after revision of man's basic beliefs in the concept of God?

Today some sit in a vast circle…stretching around the world…seeing and not seeing the view of the one directly beside them…seeing but not seeing the complete view of our immediate neighbor…seeing from a slightly different angle…never seeing exactly what is viewed from another position.

Some sit in square formations…four sides… four views…four sides...facing and opposing. In this formation each side sees opposition…opposition in the front and opposition on each side.

Some sit in the middle of a circle…looking at others…searching for a place to fit…looking to be included in this circle…waiting and wanting to belong…to be part of the circle…regardless of the cost.

Opposition to a race...a creed..a color or a religion...and always...but always...opposition to the rights of you...woman...any woman..all women.

Will you take that step as I have...will you leave the circle...and walk with me...man...any man...all men...as we search for the gate that we originally passed through. For only then will the true meaning of man and woman return in our life

For you and I…man and woman…woman and man must begin to stand together…side by side… facing the unknown together.

We will not form into circles…we will not form into squares…and we will not sit in the middle waiting to find a place…for my God…your God…our God has already assigned us our destiny.

And that destiny is not to be found in the conflicting words of religious scripture…for the language of God can not be recorded or deciphered unless it is done through the heart of an individual...for God...your God...my God...our God is within us all.

God's word can not be found in mass meetings or at gatherings at man made holy places where weapons of destruction are the norm....for these gatherings will not allow us to think...to pray...and to have peace of mind, for holy lands needing to be protected by the gun can not be holy. For these holy lands are holy to only a few and serve as a funeral ground for others.

For my mind tells me that God would not allow any religion that utilized the sword to establish it's self as the path to the one true God!

If it is God that we seek...we must come together...you and I...man and woman...woman and man.

We are both guilty...so let us start this love affair anew as we attempt to correct our injustices to each other...as we attempt to restore God's original plan. For when we find our true bliss and share this with our mate...you and I...man and woman...woman and man...we will invoke envy and discomfort but it will be the guideline for all of humankind in the eyes of God. For in times of stress we will use our friendship as the binding force when daily stress diminishes our romance and passion.

This binding force of friendship will allow the forces of passion and romance to simmer below the surface...but will not allow it to die.

20
THE BEGINNING

an was man before he loved..help man love and you make him a better man.

For I am a stranger and I have come to make love to you.

You have had extreme patience with my rambling for that is what it was. I ramble as ancient man has rambled... not sure of my meanings...not sure of my thoughts...not sure that you will understand. I ramble because my history or my grammar is probably not correct. I ramble because that is all that I can do when I attempt to begin to comprehend that which I believe is totally incomprehensible.

I know that we again stand outside of the gates of a new opportunity...a new garden…a new hope, and the choice is now truly ours…together...you and I...man and woman...woman and man.

I will write again as my travels reveal the depth of your sleep. I will write hopeful that you will contribute to this awakening of man and woman… woman and man.

The last chapter must be written by you and I... man and woman…woman and man and the hand of God as it was supposed to be in the beginning…and together... **we will be strangers no more.**

CREDITS

MOTHER AND CHILD

Original oil painting by
Yolanda Woodberry

COVER
MAN AND WOMAN...WOMAN AND MAN
MASK OF FEAR
MATING GAME
ANCIENT GODS
MATING DRUM
THE IMAGE OF LUST
A DIFFERENT VEIW
COURTSHIP
SURROGATES
THE BEARER OF LIFE
THE CLIFF

Original acrylic paintings by
Warren Woodberry

****

**My gratitude to Ms. Becky Bowlander,
Assistant Director of Writing at
Toledo University, for assisting with the
editing and proofreading.
A most difficult task.**

293

About the author

Warren Woodberry has lived in the country of Antigua/Barbuda in the West Indies with his artist wife Yolanda for the past 18 years. His claims to fame are being the son of Alice Woodberry of Toledo Ohio, being the husband of Yolanda, being blessed with four beautiful grandchildren, Tyrrell, Alecia, Xavier and Sharonnie, and having lived through his younger days.

His first book reflects his deep concern for the relationships exhibited between men and women and the lack of understanding and commitment needed to sustain a meaningful relationship, which in some cases are complicated by numerous attempts to decipher the meanings of religious texts which basically seek to show that women are second class citizens throughout the world.
Warren feels that these interpretations were done by men that had experienced very little love or contact with early women, hence they sought to establish religious scriptures that dealt very harshly with the subject of the relationship of women and men.

Warren contends that it is unimaginable that a loving God would decree the type of retaliation and treatment against women that can be found in many religious scriptures throughout the world, still in existence today, and in some small way he hopes that this book will begin a new dialogue between man and woman...and woman and man.